Inside the Cold War

A Cold Warrior's Reflections

Chris Adams

Air University Press
Maxwell Air Force Base, Alabama

September 1999

Library of Congress Cataloging-in-Publication Data

Adams, Chris, 1930–
    Inside the Cold War : a cold warrior's reflections / Chris Adams.
       p.   cm.
    Includes bibliographical references and index.
    1. Adams, Chris, 1930– . 2. United States. Air Force—Generals
Biography. 3. Strategic forces—United States Biography.
I. Title.
UG626.2.A33A33   1999
358.4′0092—dc21
[B]   99 37305
                                                 CIP

ISBN 1-58566-068-X

Disclaimer

Dedicated to the Cold Warriors

I hesitate to wonder where our country and our freedoms would be today if it were not for the hard work, sacrifice, and commitment of our Cold War combat crews. The free world is indebted to them, and to those who came before them.

Contents

Foreword

The term "Cold War" was first used in public by Winston Churchill, speaking at Westminster College in Fulton, Missouri, in March 1946. The Department of Defense has recently defined the period of the conflict from 2 September 1945, the date Japan formally surrendered after World War II, to 26 December 1991, when Mikhail Gorbachev resigned as Soviet president and the Soviet Union was disbanded. The Cold War was a significant historical anomaly for the United States. We had never fought a war over such an extended period—more than 40 years. Downsizing after such a lengthy time was very painful because, for the first time in our recent history, everyone in uniform was a volunteer when the conflict was over . . . and never had so many served in fighting a war. An estimated 22 million men and women were engaged in one way or another.

While a significant number of our military forces were engaged with the Soviet Union, the warriors in the front lines day in and day out were the members of the Strategic Air Command . . . known simply as SAC by most. The command stood up in March 1946, with 37,000 warriors, peaked with almost 283,000 men and women in 1962, and was disbanded with the stand-up of the United States Strategic Command in June 1992.

I can think of no one more qualified or prepared to tell the Cold War story than Maj Gen Christopher S. Adams, USAF, Retired. In the trenches as a bomber pilot and missile crew member for most of his career, he was part of that professional group expected to perform flawlessly on every mission, simulator ride, or alert tour. A tough but compassionate leader, Chris was one of the most respected, revered, and effective wing and air division commanders in the history of SAC. His leadership footprints are still visible in the halls of US Strategic Command even today. He has a rare talent for unbiased observation, an uncanny ability to cut through the chaff, and the savvy to tell a gripping story. This book, *Inside the Cold War*, tells that story, in my view, better than anything published to date.

We fought the Cold War with hundreds of thousands of dedicated professionals like Capt Chris Adams . . . we won the Cold War because of the extraordinary leadership and vision of a relatively few senior officers like Maj Gen Christopher Adams.

Eugene E. Habiger
General, USAF, Retired
Commander in Chief
US Strategic Command
(1996–1998)

About the Author

Christopher (Chris) S. Adams Jr. was born in Shreveport, Louisiana, on 8 July 1930. He grew up in Texas and entered Air Force pilot training in August 1952, following graduation and commissioning from the Air Force Reserve Officer Training Corps program at East Texas State University (now Texas A & M University - Commerce). Pilot training was followed by 13 years of SAC combat crew duty—first as a B-36 pilot with the 95th Bomb Wing, Biggs Air Force Base (AFB), Texas, then as a B-52G pilot at Ramey in Puerto Rico. Several Chromedome missions later, and after the Cuban crisis, General Adams attended missile combat crew training. Upon completion of missile crew training, he was assigned to the 44th Strategic Missile Wing (SMW), Ellsworth AFB, South Dakota, as a Minuteman combat crew commander and the wing senior instructor crew commander. Vietnam brought him back to the cockpit as a C-141 transport pilot at Dover AFB, Delaware, in support of Southeast Asia (SEA) operations. Later, he was reassigned to the combat zone as Director of Operations, 388th Combat Support Group at Korat Air Base, Thailand.

Following his SEA tour, General Adams was assigned to Joint Task Force Eight (Defense Nuclear Agency [DNA]), Sandia Base, New Mexico, as the air operations officer for atmospheric nuclear readiness-to-test planning. From Sandia Base, he was assigned to DNA Headquarters in Washington, D.C., first as executive to the director and later as Director, J-5. Following his DNA tour, he moved in quick succession from deputy commander for operations to vice commander and then commander of a SAC Minuteman Missile Wing.

Selected for promotion to brigadier general in November 1975, Chris Adams assumed command of 12th Air Division, which included two B-52 wings, a U-2 wing, and a Titan II ICBM wing. In July 1976, he was directed to move 12th Air Division Headquarters to Dyess AFB, Texas, and to begin preparations for accepting the B-1 bomber. However, the election of Jimmy Carter in November brought a temporary cancellation of the B-1. President Reagan restored the B-1 program in 1981.

General Adams proceeded to Headquarters SAC, as deputy director of operations. Following this assignment, General Adams served as deputy chief of staff, Operations - Plans, and as deputy director, Joint Strategic Target Planning Staff. In June 1982, he became chief of staff, SAC.

General Adams retired with 8,000 flying hours, 1,100 of which were in SEA operations. His decorations include the Distinguished Service Medal, the Department of Defense Superior Service Medal, the Legion of Merit w/1OLC, the Meritorious Service Medal, the Air Medal w/1OLC, the Air Force Commendation Medal w/3OLCs, and the Combat Crew Medal. When he retired from active duty in February 1983, Chris Adams became associate director of Los Alamos National Laboratory. He joined Andrew Corporation in March 1986, as vice president for business development. He worked extensively in various areas of the former Soviet Union from 1991 through 1995, directing the recovery of their near-collapsed commercial communications systems.

General Adams has been honored as a Distinguished Alumnus of both Tarleton State University and Texas A & M University – Commerce, and is a graduate of both Industrial College of the Armed Forces and Naval Postgraduate School. He has published articles in several professional journals, including the *Air University Digest, Combat Crew Magazine,* and *The Journal of Electronic Defense.*

Acknowledgments

Someone once said there is a book in each of us just waiting to be written. Perhaps it was also said, "*The gestation period can be a **very** long time!*"

I had this "bug" buzzing around in my head for several years before I gathered the courage to let it out. But for the overwhelming encouragement and suggestions I received from friends, colleagues, leaders, mentors, and many other Cold Warriors I had never met, I would likely never have done it.

In the post-Cold War era, I have been fortunate to travel extensively within the former Soviet Union, and within states that had formerly been part of the Soviet Union, making some 23 extended visits. These visits provided personal reflections and opinions relative to the "defeated" Soviets and their former allies. I was privileged to witness, and even to participate in, some of their attempts to recover. I am deeply grateful to the many acquaintances I made in those regions and wish to express my sincere thanks to them for their friendship and candor.

I am especially indebted to: Bonita Bradshaw; Vice Adm Jon L. Boyes, PhD, USN, Retired; Brig Gen William R. Brooksher, USAF, Retired; Lt Gen Richard A. Burpee, USAF, Retired; Vice Adm Kenneth Carr, USN, Retired; Gen Russell E. Dougherty, USAF, Retired; Lt Gen James V. Edmundson, USAF, Retired; Maj Gen James C. Enney, USAF, Retired; Lt Gen Lincoln D. Faurer, USAF, Retired; CMSGT John F. Forgette, USAF, Retired; Lt Gen Edgar S. Harris Jr., USAF, Retired; Col Larry Hasbrouk, PhD, USAF, Retired; Gen Robert T. Herres, USAF, Retired; Comdr Bill Hulvershorn, USN, Retired; Lt Gen Warren D. Johnson, USAF, Retired; Vice Adm Robert Y. "Yogi" Kaufman, USN, Retired; Maj Gen James B. Knapp, USAF, Retired; Col Alvin J. Lebsack, USAF, Retired; Lt Col Wilson E. Main, USAF, Retired; Vice Adm Jerry E. Miller, USN, Retired; Col John T. Moser, USAF, Retired; Carol Moser; Col William F. Moses, USAF, Retired; Maj Gen Earl G. Peck, USAF, Retired; Brig Gen Allen K. Rachel, PhD, USAF, Retired; Brig Gen Walter B. Ratliff, USAF, Retired; Phoebe S. Spinrad, PhD; Rear

Adm Paul Tomb, USN, Retired; and Rear Adm Ross N. Williams, USN, Retired. As this publication goes to press, I wish to join other comrades-in-arms in acknowledging the passing of Maj Gen "Jim" Knapp, *steely-eyed* warrior, leader, and artful contributor to this piece.

I am also indebted to dozens of others who simply said, "Do it." Finally, I wish to acknowledge all of those whom I met in the former Soviet Union for the opportunity to dialogue and debate the issues. I am sincerely grateful to everyone who contributed thoughts and ideas—Cold Warriors all!

Introduction

This publication reflects a compilation of excerpts from an unpublished broader treatment that recounts the nearly five decades of delicate coexistence between two nations known as the "superpowers" during the international conflict known as the "Cold War." Publication of this text fulfills one of my principal purposes in the original manuscript; that is, to pay tribute to that special breed of American heroes known as the "Cold Warriors"—the men and women who served in the strategic nuclear forces during the Cold War. Another purpose is to provide a brief parallel view of Soviet war fighters. These two opposing groups of warriors served their respective countries faithfully during those critical years of roller coaster politics, inconsistent diplomacy, and occasional lunacy.

The Cold Warriors were the centerpiece of that protracted conflict; many paid the supreme price. This text attempts to provide a reasonably comprehensive essay on the Cold Warriors—both American and Soviet—their commitments, their weapon systems, their missions, and their sacrifices. It has been said that war is faceless; the Cold War represents a time when two nations created unprecedented arsenals and stood ready to attack, or be attacked by, the faceless enemy. The United States and the Soviet Union maintained that unprecedented mutual stance over a sustained period of time.

There were a series of critical events during this *war*, including the Berlin Blockade, the invasions of Hungary and Czechoslovakia, the Korean and Cuban crises, and the war in Vietnam. All involved the Cold Warriors in one way or another. They were often called upon to transition from their primary strategic nuclear combat preparation role into totally different mission environments and war-fighting systems. These transitions required retraining and reorientation as well as relocating. Then they returned to their original strategic nuclear mission—which required still more retraining, reorientation, and relocating.

Many sources were used in the preparation of this journal, but the most numerous by far were unpublished materials, personal interviews, and my own experiences and observations. It was in fact the enthusiastic interest and cooperation of many professionals, some of whom were my colleagues in arms, that made this project possible. It is to those colleagues, and others who so honorably served, that all credit should be given.

A former Cold Warrior colleague commented, upon hearing that I was off on this writing venture, "If you are going to make an omelet, you are going to have to break a few eggs in the process." Indeed, I have undoubtedly broken a few eggs in expressing my opinions. I hope you enjoy the omelet.

Chris Adams

Chapter 1

The Cold Warriors

Through the potential power and flexibility of this equipment, and the skilled hands and minds of you and crew members like you throughout our commands, the leaders of our country and the allied nations are assured of the backdrop of credible military power to stand up to and overcome any hostile threat . . . any form of intimidation or coercion.

—Gen Russell E. Dougherty
Commander in Chief
Strategic Air Command
15 November 1975

Rumors had been circulating within the 95th Bomb Wing for the better part of a year. One day soon, it was said, Strategic Air Command (SAC) is going to place combat crews and their bombers and tankers on ground alert. If that were true, we would be required to "camp out" somewhere on base near our aircraft for indeterminate hours, days, or weeks—and to be continuously prepared to fly a preplanned mission to a target in the Soviet Union. The alert bombers would always be standing ready, loaded with nuclear weapons corresponding to the designated targets in our mission folder, and the tankers would be prepared to refuel the B-47s and B-52s.

As the rumors heated up, we heard that the old base operations building on the flight line was being refurbished to house ground alert crews. Some of the more curious of us made a special trip by the facility one day and found that the perimeter of the building was being enclosed with a ten-foot-high chain-link fence topped with a coil of razor wire. The area took on the appearance more of a mini-incarceration facility than a "hostel" for SAC's elite combat crews. The only observed clue to suggest otherwise was that the top of the fence flared out. This arrangement was a reasonable clue that it was meant to keep intruders out rather than insiders in. The senior officers in the wing kept quiet about the impending change in the lives of thousands of men, women, and their families until the

"D-Day" announcement finally came: SAC combat crews would be placed on ground alert as of 1 October 1957.

The United States had become increasingly concerned with the mounting progress the Soviets were making in developing intercontinental ballistic missile (ICBM) technology. The threat of incoming ICBM warheads on US military installations and airfields led the military planners to determine that SAC could have as little as 15 minutes to get its bomber force airborne after detection of an incoming ICBM re-entry vehicle (RV). The only way to assure reasonable success in launching a retaliatory strike force would be to place as many bombers and tankers on fast-reaction alert as could be managed. Ground alert feasibility tests, conducted with two bomber and two tanker units during the past year, had found the alert concept operationally feasible, but there was a major shortfall: insufficient ground and flight crew manning to support a sustained ground alert operation. While the many details were still being worked out, the ground alert began on 1 October, just three days before sputnik alarmed the world. The ground alert status would eventually require that one-third of the entire SAC combat-ready bomber and tanker force be on continuous 15-minute alert response time.

Joining the SAC force in this new call to duty, professionalism, discipline, hard work, and sacrifice was the nuclear submarine Navy. The nuclear submarines, which came along in the early 1960s, also met the challenge—first with Polaris, then Poseidon, and finally Trident sea-launched ballistic missiles (SLBM). Their alert posture called for remaining submerged at sea for periods of 60 days or more, constantly ready to launch missiles.

Although attention was focused on the many who wore flight suits, missile combat crew uniforms, and nuclear submariner uniforms, thousands of support men and women served on aircraft ground crews, submarine tenders, and maintenance crews. Often overlooked, these warriors also served, as did thousands of staff "weenies," many of whom had "graduated" from the combat crew force; they continued to work, often even harder.

Finally, the really great feature of national strength that evolved during the four and one-half decades of the Cold War were the young "Cold Warriors" who went on to become distinguished commanders and leaders. The Cold War period witnessed the growth and elevation of many who clearly equaled the leadership and competence of the great heroes of World Wars I and II. Among those Cold Warriors was Gen Russell E. Dougherty. Revered by all who served under him, General Dougherty often referred to himself as the first "non-hero" to command SAC. However, he indeed *was* a hero to those he led.

The Cold Warriors will always be remembered for their extraordinary patriotism, dedication, and personal sacrifice in the cause of freedom. They came to serve from all walks of life—small towns and large cities, farms and ranches, small high schools and large universities. They were remarkable young men and women who voluntarily became pilots, navigators, crew chiefs, gunners, missile crew members, submariners, maintenance specialists, logisticians, and administrative stalwarts. They matured more quickly and professionally than their civilian counterparts could ever imagine, and they took on awesome responsibilities far earlier in their lives than did those in any other career field. The young Cold Warrior's career horizon was often only a few months away—sometimes just beyond the next sortie or mission. Consequently, the Cold Warrior force remained remarkably young. They met rigorous standards of performance at every job level. The Strategic Air Command's hard-earned reputation for efficiency and excellence became the envy of all the military services. Adm Thomas Moorer, when he was Chairman of the Joint Chiefs of Staff in 1971, commented that "SAC enjoys world-wide the reputation of being the ultimate in professionalism and readiness and it has set the standard for all the military organizations of the world." And General Dougherty, in a 1992 talk, concluded ". . . [SAC's standards alone] had one 'helluva' lot to do with our effective deterrence for over 40 years. SAC's capability was real—and the world knew it! SAC's story is a success story of monumental dimensions—and you [combat crews] made it so! You made it that way—and you kept it that way."

In no way do I wish to neglect or offend any of the many other military men and women who served their country during those challenging years. Among them are my many friends in tactical air units, North American Aerospace Defense Command (NORAD) and Air Defense Command, Military Airlift Command, and the Army Nike air defense and Pershing intermediate-range ballistic missile (IRBM) units. Also among them are the Cold Warriors aboard carriers, destroyers, battleship task forces, and tactical submarines—Cold Warriors all. I will stay within the bounds of my knowledge and experience, however, and limit this review principally to the undeniable backbone of US Cold War deterrence—the men and women of our strategic nuclear forces.

I often marveled at our Cold War leaders' cleverly articulated analogies; they had a way of reducing the world's complex and critical situations to common sense. One such metaphor, expressed by General Dougherty, was, "_capability_ x _will_ = _deterrence._" He noted that if either of the multiplication factors in the equation was zero, then the product would be zero. Capability was the US strategic forces—the Triad that constituted the "three legs" of the US military's strategic nuclear deterrence. Strategic Air Command operated two legs—the bomber force and the land-based ICBM force. The Navy operated the third leg—the nuclear submarine fleet ballistic missile (SSBN) force. The capability factor also included air refueling tankers and airborne reconnaissance platforms. US capability was undeniably awesome. The will factor reflected the will of the nation and the national command authorities (NCA). _If either factor were zero, then the product would be zero._

If I were to embellish his equation in any way, it would be to add one component—that of _perception._ During the Cold War, perceptions were frequently as important as realities. Perceptions were, perhaps, the "essence" of deterrence—perceptions by Americans, by our allies, and by the Soviets. The American people took faith in the perceived capabilities of our strategic nuclear might. Our allies maintained their perception of America as the defender of freedom and oppression. And, importantly, Soviet perceptions of our capabilities—and our will to use those capabilities—kept them in check. The United States wove its way along an evolving and uneven path, often critical, from the end of World War II and the beginning of the Cold War to the "end of the Soviet Empire." More often than not, the path was strewn with political considerations, budgetary realities, new theories, and the ever-present specter of Soviet intentions. Few would dispute that the unwavering will and support of the American people, through almost two generations, claimed the Cold War victory.

Someone along the way said that if the United States had set out to develop a deterrent military force, the Triad would, in all likelihood, not have been devised. Triad was simply the result of "politics, budgetary realities, and new theories." But it worked!

Strategic Flexibility

The clock radio on the nightstand beside the bed reflected 4:00 a.m. and the intervening three or four seconds seemed like an eternity before I realized that the incessant ringing was not the alarm, but the telephone. I answered the phone with a poorly disguised attempt to sound fully awake—until the tense voice of the wing command post controller relayed the information that this *was not* a practice alert notification. Practice alert phone calls were the norm in SAC; they could be expected at any time, day or night—especially at night. Some alert notifications were simply to run the "pyramid alert" call list for confirmation of crew members' availability and then tell the sleepy warriors to go back to bed. Other notifications required crew members to hustle to their bomb squadrons, conduct a quick study of their strike mission folder, preflight their assigned aircraft, start engines, and taxi toward the runway before the alert was called off. More often than not, the wary bomber or tanker crew did not know for sure if the alert was real until the command post called off the exercise.

On this early morning occasion, the command post controller made it clear that this was not a practice; a situation briefing was scheduled for 0530 to issue the operations order. Bomb wing personnel had been placed on restriction for the past three days because of Soviet Red Army activities in Hungary, so the alert was not entirely unexpected (at least to test the bomb wing's reaction time). But this call was not for a reaction check.

A million things can run through your mind as you proceed through the routine of getting into a flight suit and collecting essentials, then driving to the base. All the things you had planned to do that day—change oil in the car, go to the cleaners, purchase an anniversary gift, get a haircut, and go out to dinner that evening—take on a much lesser meaning.

My B-36 crew's mission, if the "balloon" had *really* gone up, would have been to deliver one or more nuclear weapon(s) on preselected targets in the Soviet Union. We would deploy from our home base at Biggs Air Force Base (AFB), Texas, to Kirtland AFB, near Albuquerque, New Mexico, where the munitions crews at the Manzano nuclear storage facility would load on the prescribed weapons for the mission. From there, we would fly to a designated forward staging base, refuel, rest if possible, and await further orders to launch a strike against petroleum and transportation facilities in western Russia. This was a 1950s scenario, and the event was real. Fortunately, the Soviets *perceived* that the United States and the Free World were serious about the prevention of further encroachment; the crisis subsided.

This reflection of a possible strategic nuclear attack, which might have happened in the late 1940s or early 1950s, was in sharp contrast to the flexibility and response of later strategic forces. As we look back 40 or so years at those prodigious but cumbersome response options to crisis situations, we find sharp contrast in comparison to the evolution of war-fighting capabilities that came along in the 1960s and thereafter. As we have seen, strategic forces were not always so capable of a wide range of employment choices—nor were they always so necessary. While the pathway I alluded to was often fraught with the realities of our democratic processes, the steady shaping and enhancing of Cold War national strategic policy resulted in flexible, well-thought-out, preplanned attack options that were closely matched with existing capabilities. Combat crew members at times found themselves overwhelmed with constant training, standardization, checklists, tactical doctrine, command and control procedures, and weapon system proficiency. Yet, they performed—and performed well. They formed the lifeblood of US Cold War fighting capability.

6

The flexible employment options continued to evolve with the ever-changing nuclear weapon employment policies that resulted from continuous shifts in the international balance of power and the growing potential threat. The United States, enjoying unquestioned strategic nuclear superiority through-out the 1950s and into the 1960s, relied for deterrence upon a policy of massive retaliation.

Strategic Air Command had been in existence since shortly after the end of World War II. Gen Carl A. Spaatz announced its establishment on 21 March 1946, while he and the new command were still part of the Army. "The Strategic Air Command will be prepared to conduct long-range offensive operations in any part of the world . . . to conduct maximum-range reconnaissance over land or sea . . . and to provide combat units capable of intense and sustained combat operations employing the latest and most advanced weapons."

Gen George C. Kenney, SAC's first commanding general, immediately began to gather the resources necessary to flesh out the command. For the first six months, SAC was headquartered at Bolling AFB in the District of Columbia. In October 1946, the headquarters moved to Andrews AFB, Maryland. The new command's charter seemed straightforward enough, but military service rivalry in the initial postwar years reached a feverish pitch as each fought for missions, budgets, and resources to maintain some semblance of military capability. The understandably jealous factions of other branches of the Army began immediately to undermine and discredit this "Phoenix" that was about to rise from the ashes of a rapidly diminishing World War II airpower capability.

Gen James M. Gavin, one of the Army's bright intellects, argued that should there be a major conflict with Russia it would be a ground army "peripheral war," and not a struggle for air supremacy. (Despite the implications in General Gavin's remark, air supremacy was not SAC's intended mission.) He called the bombing of Hiroshima and Nagasaki "indiscriminate" and said that such a tactic in Eastern Europe would poison the land for generations. He further argued that SAC had no charter to claim strategic targets in Russia or anywhere else. The Joint Chiefs of Staff (JCS), of course, had already approved an initial SAC-devised plan to strike targets deep inside Russia if war became inevitable.

Others in the Army argued that surface-to-air missiles such as the US Nike would be capable of shooting down bombers (even supersonic ones) or missiles in any future conflict. And, they argued, the Russians would certainly have that capability. Gen Maxwell Taylor did not approve creation of such a strategic war-fighting command with so much authority. He argued that properly deployed Redstone and Pershing IRBMs could contain any Soviet breakout in Europe and support the infantry as it fought an advancing Red Army.

The airpower debate continued even as SAC began to develop its capabilities and strategies, sensitive to—but undaunted by—the sharp critics. Critics of airpower's rise were also prominent in the Soviet Union. Stalin, for example, denounced the development of Soviet airpower and declared that wars were fought and won on the ground with artillery and infantry. Also entering the fight for mission assignment and recognition was the Navy. Adm Arleigh Burke, chief of Naval Operations, argued that: "mutually opposing, poised long-range aerial fleets, designed for use only with 'ultimate weapons,' can hardly be usable or useful in meeting local emergency situations which historically have been the seeds of large-scale war." Admiral Burke also claimed that the Navy, "carrying hydrogen bombs that can be delivered today, may under certain circumstances deliver more bruising blows much more quickly than SAC."

In speaking against building the B-36 and the notion of the heavy all-jet B-52 in the future, Rear Adm James Russell, chief of the Navy Bureau of Aeronautics, argued that the Navy's prototype jet seaplane, the P6M, could be more effective than land-based bombers. "Sea planes could also 'hide' in ocean coves and inlets around the world and be supported by ship task forces." The P6M, however, was completely incapable of carrying the size and weight of the early nuclear (atomic) weapons.*

---

*The terms *atomic* and *nuclear* are interchangeable; I will generally refer to atomic bombs as the early weapons and nuclear weapons as the later ones.

The arguments persisted; they got very nasty and very public, finally resulting in the ill-famed "Admiral's Revolt." Meanwhile, SAC continued to build the controversial B-36 and plan for a future all-jet bomber force supplemented with ICBMs. The command had begun with only 148 B-29 bombers, two fighter squadrons of P-51s to be employed as escorts, and 15 C-54s to haul supporting cargo. As the first year of postwar confusion subsided, the number of recovered B-29s increased to more than three hundred.

The arguments for and against long-range strategic forces continued for years—and not only in Washington. Early in 1955, Field Marshal Bernard L. Montgomery gave his assessment of organizing for war: "The fleets at sea-in-being may be the only undamaged echelon in the armed forces after the initial clash." Winston Churchill, a staunch supporter of US war-fighting skills, countered his old wartime military leader in a speech to Parliament in the spring of that year: "The United States Strategic Air Command is a deterrent of the highest order in maintaining ceaseless readiness. We owe much to their devotion to the cause of freedom in a troubled world. The primary deterrents to aggression remain the nuclear weapon and trained United States Strategic Air Command [combat crews] to use it."

During its first eleven years, SAC enjoyed virtual supremacy in the international skies. Its round-the-world flights demonstrated its capability to reach anywhere on the face of the earth. Within weeks of its official establishment, the command began training with, and learning the intricacies of employing, atomic weapons. SAC was given an opportunity to "test" deterrence in November, when it was directed to send six B-29s to Rhein-Main, Germany, because two US C-47 cargo planes had been shot down over Yugoslavia by Soviet forces. During their two-week deployment, the B-29s flew along the borders of Soviet-occupied political eastern Europe and landed in several western European cities, essentially sending a message to the Soviets that the United States was not abandoning its allies. The B-29s likely did not pose an ominous threat to the Soviets, but their reputation as atomic bomb delivery aircraft conveyed a strong message.

Lt Gen Curtis E. LeMay, commander of US Air Forces in Europe, called upon the B-29s again in June 1948, at the outset of the Berlin Blockade. Later that year, on 19 October, General LeMay was named commanding general of SAC; the "era of SAC" had begun in earnest.

Earlier in 1946, President Harry S. Truman had approved Operation Crossroads, an exercise designed to evaluate the destructive, radiation, and collateral effects of atomic weapons. The exercise involved over 42,000 SAC, Navy, and civilian scientists. On 1 July 1946, in the first exercise event, a B-29 crew commanded by Maj (later Maj Gen) Woodrow P. Swancutt dropped a Nagasaki-type bomb at Bikini Atoll in the South Pacific. The planned air detonation exploded over 73 target ships of various types moored off Bikini. Five ships sank immediately and nine were badly damaged. The Navy then detonated a second atomic device that was tethered under water, beneath a landing ship transport (LST) craft; it caused even greater damage to the targeted surface ships. The success of these two detonations led to cancellation of a planned third blast.

The Defense Department and the scientific community had determined that the testing of atomic-type weapons warranted the requirement that specially trained people, beyond SAC and Navy crews, conduct such experiments. Accordingly, the Atomic Energy Commission (AEC), forerunner to the present Department of Energy, was created as a civilian agency and the Armed Forces Special Weapons Project (AFSWP – "Af-Swop") was established as the military agency to jointly coordinate nuclear activities. AEC was charged with principal responsibility for the design and development of nuclear weapons, providing the budgets, and managing the contracts of the national nuclear-related laboratories. AFSWP was charged with coordinating the planning of nuclear weapons tests, conducting research on nuclear effects, and providing technical, logistical, and training support for the Department of Defense (DOD) testing units.

Maj Gen Leslie Groves, who had headed-up the Manhattan Project, was appointed director of AFSWP. In time, and following mission charter adjustments, AFSWP was renamed Defense Atomic Support Agency (DASA) in 1959. In 1971, it became the Defense Nuclear Agency (DNA); finally, in 1996, it became the Defense Special Weapons Agency (DSWA). Atmospheric and, later, underground tests of nuclear devices were conducted jointly by these agencies to validate performance, safety, reliability, and destructive/radiation effects. The military services and the national laboratories provided the necessary resources and technical support for the testing. I was fortunate to be assigned for a time to Joint Task Force Eight (JTF-8), the field planning and testing unit of DASA and DNA, headquartered at Sandia Base, New Mexico, and later as a staff officer at DNA Headquarters in Washington, D.C. This was a rare and exceptional opportunity for a Cold Warrior to work alongside the nuclear weapons scientists/designers from Los Alamos, Livermore, and Sandia laboratories. Also, I was able to participate in weapons test planning, and in exercises. Many of the original atomic bomb scientists, engineers, and technicians, some of whom became legends within their own time, remained active in the weapons development program into the 1960s and 1970s. Nuclear weapons testing continued in the South Pacific, directed from the elaborate test and monitoring facilities located on Johnston Atoll, six hundred miles south of the Hawaiian Islands. Following the signing of the Atmospheric Test Ban Treaty in July 1963, all nuclear weapons testing went underground at the Nevada Test Site near Mercury, Nevada. By that time, the United States and the Soviet Union had conducted a total of 336 nuclear weapons tests in the 17 years since the end of World War II.

Following its establishment and during the decade of the 1950s, SAC enjoyed a swift evolution of weapon systems and strategic tactics. The controversial B-36 bomber came and went, replaced by the B-52. The B-47, B-58, Atlas, and Titan I were phased out in the mid-1960s. Atlas II, Minuteman, and Titan II replaced Atlas and Titan I, eventually comprising a combined total of 1,054 ICBMs by the mid-1960s.

The last generation of Minuteman (MM III) brought an enhanced flexibility to the SAC force through multiple independently targetable re-entry vehicle (MIRV) payloads and a command data buffer, which allowed rapid retargeting from the Minuteman launch control centers. The added capabilities increased the targeting and war-fighting utility of the SAC forces. Air-launched missiles such as Hound Dog and short-range attack missile (SRAM) extended target coverage and allowed the B-52s to more efficiently attack heavily defended targets in the Soviet Union. The SRAM, with its supersonic speed, selectable yields, and multiple flight profiles, was as significant to SAC's flexibility and capability as was the jet engine and air refueling in earlier years. As the Minuteman I missiles phased out in 1974, SAC's force level and war-fighting capability remained unchanged with the introduction of Minuteman III and the MK12A warhead—three in each missile RV, with twice the bomb yield of the older warheads. The late 1970s and the 1980s brought the MX ICBM, with its greater silo survivability and improved capability against the full range of Soviet targets, and the air-launched cruise missile (ALCM), which gave the B-52 force greater flexibility in planning, penetration, and survivability. The dramatic and decisive evolution of strategic war-fighting capabilities was paralleled closely by the nuclear submarine SLBM force development, enhanced reconnaissance capabilities, sophisticated intelligence techniques, and survivable command, control, and communications systems.

Survivable and enduring communications were the "heart and soul" of ensuring that the ground, airborne, and ICBM alert forces received transmitted execution orders if and when initiated. The first emergency "backup" communications system was the Blue Scout rocket program. Initiated in July 1963 at three operational launch sites in central Nebraska, Blue Scout was designed to augment the SAC underground post. Blue Scout's small rockets, equipped with ultra high frequency (UHF) recorder-transmitters, would be launched to high altitudes for broadcasting authenticated execution messages to SAC forces. Later, selected Minuteman missiles equipped with emergency rocket communications system (ERCS) voice recorder-transmitters replaced the Blue Scout system. During the late 1970s, Gen Richard H. Ellis, SAC commander, became increasingly concerned about the survivability of the critical communications links that would be necessary in the event of a nuclear attack. Test results from atmospheric detonation of nuclear weapons in the Pacific clearly showed that most existing communications systems were vulnerable to blackout periods lasting from minutes to hours.

Since detonation of an antiballistic (ABM) warhead in the atmosphere could "knock out" communications over the United States, General Ellis initiated a comprehensive study of the various effects on command and control communications during deployments of strategic forces in wartime. The results of the study prompted the JCS to create the Joint Strategic Connectivity Staff (JSCS), which would be collocated with SAC Headquarters at Offutt AFB. The CINCSAC would be JSCS director; a rear admiral would be vice director and chief operating officer.

The purpose of JSCS was to analyze strategic connectivity systems and procedures for SAC "readiness." There were many dimensions to the SAC's forces and alert postures—policy, analysis, planning, continuous evaluation of both threat and personnel—and the third leg of the Triad, the nuclear-powered strategic ballistic missile submarine (SSBN), became operational in the early 1960s. After analyzing these myriad components, JSCS would make recommendations to the Joint Chiefs.

During the 1950s, the Navy began to seriously investigate the feasibility of launching large missiles from submarines. The furor over the "missile gap" and Soviet advances in SSBN and SLBM development hastened their investigation and stimulated the availability of money for the pursuit. The major questions were how to design missile size and propulsion to "fit" into a submarine and how to acquire the ability to safely launch it. Atlas, Titan, and Minuteman were not feasible because of their size. Further, the volatile liquid propellants of Atlas and Titan could not be considered for submarine use.

Even a more moderate version of any available system would require horizontal storage aboard the submarine and a launch pad on the sub's surface. Other considerations were the potential for enlarging the basic submarine size and maintaining buoyancy after a missile launch. A missile launch from beneath the surface immediately extracts thousands of pounds from a submerged boat, causing a sudden shift in transfer of buoyant weight—and the principle of submarine technology revolves around the delicate balance between positive and negative buoyancy. The Navy, however, *had* to get into the strategic nuclear business or be left behind. The Air Force, SAC in particular, was moving ahead rapidly with long-range heavy bombers and ICBMs along with the budget priorities to support them. Long-range submersible systems, capable of deceptive maneuvering with multiple ICBMs that could strike strategic targets, was the obvious direction to pursue.

During World War II, the Soviets had built the largest fleet of submarines in the world. As the Cold War evolved, they continued to build submarines—and to improve their technologies. NATO feared that the Soviets would block all European sea lanes and threaten continental facilities with their fleet of three hundred or more submarines, some of which were armed with ballistic missiles. The Soviets began their SLBM program in 1955, converting six *Zulu*-class diesel submarines into boats that could carry and launch two nuclear SS-N-4 missiles. They continued to develop diesel-electric submarines for SLBM delivery into the early 1960s, with the *Golf*-class boat capable of carrying SS-N-5s, 6s, or 8s. In 1957, they developed nuclear-propelled *Hotel*-class boats equipped with SS-N-5 and SS-N-8 SLBMs.

The US Navy pressed on with nuclear-powered submarine development. In the interim, the Navy modified several older diesel boats to launch the Regulas missile with a nuclear warhead. To accommodate the Regulas, the submarines were outfitted with a small hangar that housed two of the missiles on the deck. The boats were placed on patrol in the northwestern Pacific, within range of selected Soviet targets. The patrol tactic for the Regulas boats called for single crews, in contrast to the dual crews later assigned to the SSBN "boomer" boats. Regulas II, a larger and faster sea-launched missile, then came along with a support program that envisioned 14 nuclear submarines. The Polaris program made better progress than predicted, however, and the planned Regulas II nuclear boats were converted to nuclear-powered attack submarines. A modified *Skipjack*-class nuclear attack boat, equipped with 16 Polaris launch tubes and renamed the USS *George Washington*, became the first true SSBN. Adm Hyman Rickover had the shipbuilder "cut" the original *Skipjack* boat, the *Scorpion*, in half and insert a 130-foot missile compartment section, extending the submarine's length to 380 feet. With the follow-on Lafayette, the length would become 425 feet.

Working against a deadline to have an SSBN on patrol in 1960, the modification program met the challenge—two Polaris A1 missiles were successfully test-fired on 20 July 1960. The new strategic capability was promptly declared operationally ready and the *George Washington* deployed on the first fleet ballistic missile (FBM) patrol, slipping out of Charleston Bay on 15 November 1960 with 16 Polaris SLBMs assigned to Soviet targets. As the era of FBM deployments of the SSBNs began, the US nuclear Triad was complete.

Chapter 2

The Leaders

There were many great leaders during the Cold War, both military and civilian, and we have already mentioned a few. However, any discussion of the Cold War would be incomplete without a more detailed tribute to two particular leaders whose long shadows stretched far behind them during that critical period. Fighting conventional thought, they overcame almost insurmountable obstacles and constraints to plan and build the greatest capabilities in history to both deter and fight a war. The visions, perceptions, and extraordinary achievements of Gen Curtis E. LeMay and Adm Hyman Rickover far exceeded those of most military leaders.

The following brief profiles are not intended in any way to constitute complete biographical stories of these two leaders. Rather, they are intended to provide short composites of two controversial and unconventional men who stood above all the rest.

General Curtis E. LeMay (1906–90)

While not the first commander of Strategic Air Command (SAC), General LeMay was its "Father" by all other distinctions. In fact, many have called him the "creator" of US strategic nuclear deterrence. Of the 13 commanders of SAC, General LeMay served the longest (nine years). He was responsible for SAC's dramatic growth—not only in size, but also in war-fighting capability through technological advances.

Born in Columbus, Ohio, in November 1906, LeMay was infatuated with flying from his earliest remembrance. He wanted very much to attend West Point, but his family had neither influence nor acquaintance with Ohio's representatives and senators. Failing to receive any responses to his letters expressing interest in an appointment, he entered Ohio State University.

LeMay was commissioned as a second lieutenant in June 1928, having been an honor graduate of the Army Reserve Officer Training Training Corp (ROTC) program. Following graduation, he attended basic training with a field artillery brigade at Fort Knox, Kentucky. Determining that the field artillery was not for him, he resigned his commission at midpoint of basic training. He then applied for appointment as an officer in the Ohio National Guard, hoping to work his way into the Army Air Corps. He received the desired National Guard appointment, only to find that he had to resign that commission in order to enter pilot training as an aviation cadet.

LeMay earned his pilot wings and was commissioned for the third time in October 1929. During the next ten years, he flew fighters and bombers in various Air Corps units in the United States and Hawaii. In 1937, four years before the United States entered World War II, he was assigned to a B-17 bomb group and became one of the most proficient pilots and navigators in the unit. Excelling at every assignment given him, LeMay was promoted rapidly. In September 1942, he took the 305th Bombardment Group to England as its commander; a year later, he was promoted to brigadier general. In March 1944, at age 38, he was promoted to major general and given command of an air division consisting of 266 B-17s and B-24s—plus an additional wing of 146 B-17s. He personally flew with his bomber crews, leading his units in all of the major bombing attacks over Germany.

LeMay was reassigned in June 1944 to the Pacific Theater, as commander of XX Bomber Command—the first "strategic air command." Given the new B-29 bombers, LeMay developed long-range bombing tactics to strike Japanese targets directly—first from airfields in China, later from the Mariana Islands. Despite the XX's devastating heavy bombing attacks and firebomb raids, the Japanese refused to surrender. Finally, XX Bomber Command was given responsibility for dropping the atomic bombs on Hiroshima and Nagasaki. LeMay had already gained "hero" status in news articles, having been featured in the New York Times, Collier's, and The New Yorker. He was also featured on the 13 August 1945 cover of Time magazine. His name and reputation became synonymous with strategic bombing tactics and professional aircrews. The story was often told that when his wife, Helen, asked him why he stayed in bombers, LeMay replied, "Fighters are fun, but bombers are important."

LeMay, turning 39 at the end of the war, was assigned to the Army Air Staff in the Pentagon as Deputy Chief of Staff for research and development. While postwar downsizing and ever-decreasing budgets were a constant battle, he fought successfully for development of new bomber and fighter systems. These included completion of the four-year-old B-36 project, work on the all-jet B-47 and B-52, and development of the F-80, F-84, and F-86 jet fighters. In October 1947, LeMay was promoted to lieutenant general and sent to command US Air Forces, Europe (USAFE). Eight months later, the Soviets blockaded Berlin—and LeMay gained renewed fame.

The Army Air Corps became a separate service on 18 September 1947. A few months later, General LeMay became commander of SAC at age 42. Being the "junior" among commanders of major commands did not deter LeMay in his drive to develop SAC into the most powerful military force in the history of the world. Having successfully commanded the XX and XXI Bomber Commands, which were greatly responsible for the defeat of Japan, and having been architect of the successful Berlin Airlift operation, he easily assumed the role of commander, SAC. Biographers attribute his toughness and hard-work ethic to his early childhood and college days. The oldest of six children in an Ohio iron worker's family, he supplemented the family income with odd jobs such as shoveling snow, delivering telegrams, tending furnaces, and managing a newspaper route. While in college, he worked in a local foundry from eight to nine hours every night, six days a week. He sometimes displayed a stony, mostly expressionless glare, which has been attributed to a sinus-caused slight paralysis in his lower right jaw and lip. In his younger days, he disguised the paralysis by smoking a pipe; later, his huge "trademark" cigars played that role. Someone said he wore the cigar like a cocked pistol.

Although SAC was already in being when LeMay took command, little had been accomplished to make it a combat-ready force. He found morale reasonably high, but professionalism and crew proficiency quite low. He did not openly criticize his predecessor, Gen George C. Kenney; rather, he praised Kenney for keeping the command intact during a difficult military downsizing period. During Kenney's watch, SAC's first two years of operation, SAC bomber crews had participated in atomic bomb tests in the Pacific, begun deployment exercises to overseas bases, and responded with B-29s to the C-47 shoot-down incident in Yugoslavia.

LeMay's immediate concerns were for combat crew professionalism and proficiency. He had a knack for poking into every nook and cranny of an organization—and an eye for "uncovering" the slightest deviations from the expected norm. This "poking" extended from the general appearance of an Air Force base to the quality and service of food in the mess hall, to the cleanliness of vehicles and airplanes, to the living conditions of enlisted personnel, and, especially, to the competence and proficiency of the combat crew force. He went to the extreme in every directional sense to impress upon his staff and unit commanders that he would not tolerate anything but the best in *everything*—from shoe shines and trouser creases to navigation and bombing accuracy. He established goals in every facet of SAC life and personally inspected their accomplishment. When he took command, SAC Headquarters was in the process of moving from Andrews AFB, Maryland to Offutt AFB, Nebraska, and into an array of 75-year-old brick buildings left over from the cavalry days of old Fort Crook. There were also a few mostly wooden structures remaining from the Martin and Boeing aircraft plant that had turned out B-26s and B-29s during the war. (It was perhaps an ironic coincidence that both the Enola Gay and Bock's Car, the B-29s that dropped the atomic weapons on Japan, had come off the assembly line at the future home of SAC.) It would be over eight years before SAC Headquarters moved into newly constructed facilities—and when the move did occur, General LeMay would enjoy the new headquarters for only a few months before moving on to the Pentagon.

SAC saw its first delivery of the B-50A and the B-36 in the months before LeMay took command. (He had worked hard to get both bombers developed during his Pentagon Air Staff tour.) General LeMay began to make SAC an elite institution even in his first year, establishing the toughest proficiency training and evaluations ever known in flying operations. He used a number of creative techniques to instill competitiveness within the combat crew force:

— bombing and navigation competition events
— "spot" promotions for combat crew members who excelled and maintained the highest levels of proficiency
— long-range demonstration flights by SAC bombers
— a war planning process that included aerial reconnaissance, intelligence collection and processing, Soviet target development, and nuclear weapons employment.

Over the next several years, SAC participated in the Korean War and received the first all-jet bomber—the B-47. General LeMay continued to drill SAC in the fundamentals of strategic air war proficiency. Long-range demonstration flights were made by B-36s to the United Kingdom and North Africa. B-29 and B-50 units also conducted rotational deployments to England, Japan, Guam, and North Africa. These combat-ready bomber units were capable of launching strike missions against any targets anywhere. In 1954, B-36 bomb wings began to rotate to Guam for 90-day ground alert tours. They, too, were ready for combat, their nuclear weapons loaded for execution. The first B-52 was delivered to SAC on 29 June 1955. In November of that year, SAC was directed to integrate ICBMs into its strategic war plans.

General LeMay departed SAC on 30 June 1957 to become Vice Chief of Staff and, later, Chief of Staff, US Air Force. A revered but controversial leader, he retired from active duty in 1964. Some, this author among them, say he was the man for the time. After his death, and in the wave of "Cold War historical revisionism," many critics maligned General LeMay. His character, intentions, motivation, policies—even his personal appearance—have come under fire from such prominent writers and journalists as Pulitzer Prize winner Richard Rhodes, Northwestern University Professor Michael Sherry, and British documentary filmmaker Paul Lashmar. Their characterizations, and wholly false accounts of events in several instances, were fabricated without them ever having met General LeMay. Nor have they ever understood the necessity for his call to arms and his leadership in a perilous time. According to one of the most bizarre accusations, LeMay was to have made a secret deal with "another general in New Mexico," under which the "other general" would "turn over control of nuclear weapons" to LeMay "for his own use in SAC." Anyone ever associated with, or knowledgeable of, the national accountability and safeguard rules for controlling and managing nuclear weapons will quickly recognize the fraudulence of such a claim. Nevertheless, the accusation went forward as fact. Another myth had LeMay secretly "ordering" clandestine spy plane missions over the Soviet Union early in the Cold War without White House knowledge—a patently absurd proposition!

Latter day critics often travel the last mile in their irreverent attempts to denigrate General LeMay (and the US military as a whole). But even LeMay's harshest critics cannot deny his great achievement in developing for his country the strongest and most enduring defense posture ever known. He did not win the Cold War single-handedly, but he was one of the principal architects of the US deterrence that brought it to an end.

Admiral Hyman G. Rickover (1900–86)

Admiral Rickover was every bit as controversial as General LeMay. Several biographers have attempted to reach into Rickover's early life and the lives of his parents, but have had little success. The admiral would seldom sit still for interviews or provide enlightenment about his background. Two different dates reflect his birth: His Naval Academy biography states that he was born on 27 January 1900; other records reflect that he was born eighteen months earlier, on 24 August 1898. By some accounts, his father immigrated to the United States in 1899; others suggest 1904. In any event, Hyman Rickover was born of Jewish parents in the small village of Makow, 50 miles north of Warsaw, Poland. His father, Abraham, a tailor, found work in New York and saved enough money to bring his family to the United States. There is no clear record of exactly when Hyman Rickover, his mother, and his older sister arrived in New York, but it is known that the family relocated to Chicago around 1908. Abraham refused to move into

Chicago's tenement housing and eventually bought an apartment building in the city's Lawndale section.

Admiral Rickover attended John Marshall High School in Chicago, graduating with honors in February 1918. While attending high school, he worked as a Western Union messenger—a job that put him in frequent contact with the Chicago office of US Representative Adolph Sabath, also a Jewish immigrant. Impressed with young Hyman, Congressman Sabath awarded him an appointment to the US Naval Academy.

Never one to make friends, Rickover remained a loner and studied hard, earning a reputation as a "grind." Shunning extracurricular activities, he finished 106th in a class of 539. At graduation he received his diploma from Assistant Secretary of the Navy, Theodore Roosevelt. In his first assignment, Rickover served as a watch officer aboard the destroyer USS *La Vallette;* a year later, he was appointed engineering officer. He found his element here, running the ship's engine room. He was a "spit and polish" supervisor and a tough taskmaster. On one cruise, his engine room crew completely overhauled the ship's engines—a job that would normally be accomplished by contractors while the ship was in dry dock.

Rickover, who loved being at sea, spent 11 of his first 17 years aboard ships. After serving aboard *La Vallette,* he was assigned to the battleship *Nevada* for two years as electrical officer. In 1927, Rickover attended postgraduate school at Annapolis. Two years later, in 1929, he earned a master's degree in electrical engineering from Columbia University. He was then accepted for submarine school and assigned to the submarine S-*9.* Later, he sailed aboard the S-*48* for three years.

In May 1946, following a series of assignments as engineering officer, commanding officer of a minesweeper, commander of a ship repair facility, and inspector general of the nineteenth fleet, he was assigned to the Bureau of Ships (BuShips) as liaison officer to the Manhattan Project at Oak Ridge, Tennessee. Now a captain, Rickover had already begun to drift away from the structure of the uniformed Navy. He had also become even more of a workaholic—a tough and frugal taskmaster who forced his staff to travel on Sundays to save duty days. To further save money for his departments, he would "sponge" from contractors or friends wherever he traveled. If that wasn't possible, he and his traveling staff stayed in the cheapest hotels available. He never wore his uniform on travel, much to the displeasure of his superiors. He was rapidly becoming a legend for both his eccentric habits and for his driving genius to get the job done—and to get it done perfectly. Errors and sloppy work were unacceptable to Admiral Rickover. He was called "ruthless," "tyrant," and worse by subordinates and colleagues alike. A "TOBR Club" developed—"tossed out by Rickover."

At Oak Ridge, Rickover immediately caught the eye of Edward Teller—an association that would greatly assist Rickover in his quest to create nuclear propulsion for ships. Although his first tutorials on nuclear power did not generate immediate enthusiasm, Rickover eventually convinced Teller and others in the atomic community that nuclear energy for ship and submarine propulsion was the future of the US Navy. Upon hearing Rickover's concept for the first time, an assembly of atomic weapons scientists agreed that nuclear propulsion might be feasible—then they told him it would take 20 years to develop a demonstration model. (It may well be that all the numerous accounts of Rickover's reaction to the time estimate are true; he already had a reputation for radical departures from the norm.)

As Rickover argued at Oak Ridge for nuclear propulsion, the Air Force was winning the budget battles for developing strategic systems—the B-36 and atomic weapons delivery in particular. Missions to hit potential strategic targets within the Soviet Union were being given to the newly created SAC, in large part because the Navy had no long-range delivery vehicles. Nevertheless, members of the Atomic Energy Commission (AEC) were not easily convinced that priority development of nuclear reactors for ship propulsion was the proper way to proceed. During those tumultuous times between World War II and the Cold War, the AEC was extremely busy developing atomic weapons for aircraft delivery.

Rickover, however, was fighting everyone who questioned the nuclear propulsion concept. His efforts found a friend in Dr. Lawrence R. Hafstad, whom he had known during his earlier assignment in the Pentagon. When Hafstad was appointed head of the AEC's atomic reactor program, Rickover wasted no time in prevailing upon him to consider organizing a Naval Reactor Program within the AEC. Adm Earle Mills, who had been impressed with Rickover while working in BuShips and who supported the nuclear propulsion concept, agreed that a naval branch should be created within AEC's Division of Reactor Development. Hafstad was convinced, and Rickover was named director of the new branch.

Rickover's assignment went largely unnoticed until seniors within the Navy and the Washington community realized that Captain Rickover had taken command of both Navy's and AEC's nuclear propulsion activities. He could now send priority requests to himself from either office, obtain instant "sign-off," and proceed on his merry way. Rickover in no way abused his positions, but he did drastically cut red tape to move the program along. He was a genius at selling ideas to AEC and industry while saving money for the Navy. He convinced Westinghouse that building smaller nuclear power plants for ship propulsion would be an ideal way to pursue the goal of building industrial nuclear power plants. Westinghouse also got on board Rickover's drive to divert fissionable materials from bombs to power reactors. The AEC and a number of influential members of Congress were delighted with a US industry sharing the new technology and creating revolutionary business potential.

Meanwhile, Captain Rickover continued to build his small empire. He took over Tempo-3, a group of prefabricated buildings set up on Constitution Avenue during the War to prevent overcrowding. He then ripped out all carpeting and other items that reflected a "cushy" Washington environment and established work schedules of 14 to 16 hours a day. Money was still scarce, but Rickover somehow managed to leach enough from the Navy and other sources to continue developing a nuclear reactor and a suitable submarine. He selected the *Nautilus* to receive the new propulsion engine.

In the late 1940s and early 1950s, Rickover began to create serious problems for himself and his programs. He had become, or perhaps had always been, a complete nonconformist. He fought convention and bureaucracy at every turn. He developed complete contempt for the conventional Navy and saw the military only as a source for getting his work done. He shunned the Navy uniform, finally giving it up altogether. Stories out of his office had it that he owned two suits—a gray baggy tweed that he wore to work every day and a blue one that he wore on trips or to special meetings. He grew more and more frustrated with the people he had to advise on the complexities of managing military nuclear reactors and nuclear-powered propulsion systems. His reputation as a notorious taskmaster and brutal interviewer of job applicants continued to grow. Interviews were "cat and mouse" games, with Captain Rickover looming like a large tiger over the small mice that were sent to him as candidates to work in his program. He threw temper tantrums, cursed at what he considered wrong answers to questions (which were often ambiguous), and generally intimidated officers and civilians alike. But, surprising to Rickover's critics, candidates kept coming—and those who were finally selected to work on the program became Rickover disciples.

His philosophical battles were equally challenging. The atomic physicists tended to "rule" over his engineers, baffling them with the magic of the atom and the complexities of their work. Rickover could see his programs grinding to a halt with the "twenty-year" program approach preached to him earlier by the physicists. He finally got the theoretical physicists together and announced that, in his opinion, "The atomic-powered submarine is *95 percent engineering* and *only five percent physics.*" And, he advised them, no one should forget it. He then gave the same instructions to the engineers. Everyone must have gotten the word because program delays due to bickering and "turf battles" all but disappeared.

Meanwhile, Captain Rickover was an officer in the United States Navy—albeit one who had not endeared himself to the Navy's senior officers. He had come up for promotion to rear admiral in 1951 and had not been selected. When his records came before the promotion board in 1952, he had the support of Navy Secretary Dan Kimball, AEC Chairman Henry Jackson, Congressman Mel Price, and numerous other influential men in Congress—but he had few supporters among the Navy's senior officers.

When Rickover was passed over for promotion a second time, which meant that retirement by mid-1953 was mandatory, the Navy's promotion system came under strong pressure from influential members in the Congress. The Senate Armed Services Committee, backed by the same committee in the House, called for inquiries. In the end, and without disturbing "the system," the Navy Secretary prevailed; the following year, the promotion board had before it a set of criteria for considering specially qualified engineering officers who had excelled in their duties. The pressures of the Navy's civilian leaders, members of Congress, and prominent news media personalities combined to force Rickover's promotion; he became a rear admiral on 1 July 1953. But he was now labeled "influential with all except the Navy," a designation that would both haunt and sustain him for another 40 years.

Rickover's hard work and perseverance paid off on 30 December 1954 when the specially designed *Nautilus,* outfitted with the first shipboard-installed nuclear propulsion power plant, was brought up to running power. And, on 17 January 1955, the *Nautilus* cast off under nuclear power with Rear Admiral Rickover standing next to his handpicked commanding officer, Eugene Wilkinson. The *Nautilus'* power plant was considered "crude" by many in the atomic energy community, but it launched the Navy and the United States into a new era of war-fighting capability. Two of Rickover's staunch supporters, Congressman Mel Price and AEC Chairman Clinton Anderson, immediately called on the Navy to design nuclear-powered submarines to carry missiles with nuclear warheads. (*Nautilus* went on to break every submarine record in existence and to exceed all expectations for endurance and speed.)

These Rickover successes led to the *Polaris* submarine and SLBM programs, which were followed by the largest submarine building program in US history—all powered by nuclear energy. Rickover was promoted to vice admiral in 1958 and became only the third Naval officer in history to be awarded the Congressional Gold Medal. (The two previous recipients were Richard E. Byrd and Ernest J. King.)

In 1961, the Navy was again preparing to retire Admiral Rickover from active duty. Senior leaders arranged a ceremony on board the *Nautilus* to present the nation's highest peace-time decoration—the Distinguished Service Medal—to him. The Navy also leaked a story to the press that he would *mandatorily* retire on or about 1 July 1962. But the Navy was foiled again; Navy Secretary John Connally announced that Admiral Rickover had been asked to stay on to complete the work he had started. President Lyndon B. Johnson initiated a series of two-year appointments to retain him on active duty. Presidents Richard M. Nixon, Gerald S. Ford, and Jimmy Carter continued these two-year appointments. The Chiefs of Naval Operations were apparently never consulted.

In 1973, a Congressional Resolution recommended to the Navy that an engineering building at the Naval Academy be named after Rickover; reluctantly, the Navy complied with the recommendation. That same year, on 3 December, in a joint Senate and House Resolution, Rickover was promoted to full admiral. So, the "twice passed over" captain whom the Navy wanted to retire and "move out of the way" became a four-star admiral.

Admiral Rickover saw his promotions only as a means to facilitate his work. A nonconformist throughout his service, he appeared at times to go out of his way to demonstrate the same. He openly criticized the Navy's senior military leadership, including Adm James L. Holloway, whom he had selected as a nuclear-Navy candidate early in his career and whose father had helped Rickover's own career.

When Holloway was selected as Chief of Naval Operations (CNO), Rickover put heavy pressure on him to make the Navy "*all* nuclear." But Holloway recognized the budgetary implications and did not support Rickover's effort. When Rickover went over Holloway's head to Congress, the CNO promptly sent a signed written statement to Capital Hill. "The issue is which advice should the Congress follow: the advice of the CNO, the senior uniformed official responsible for the readiness of naval forces now and in the future, or the advice of Admiral Rickover." Holloway made his point regarding "chain of command," but several congressmen made speeches chiding the Navy for conspiring to get rid of Admiral Rickover.

Holloway's predecessor as CNO, Adm Elmo Zumwalt, had applied for the nuclear Navy as a lieutenant commander and had endured Rickover's legendary interviews. He later decided to take a different route in his career. As CNO, he had a continuous battle with the "little Admiral." Rickover challenged Zumwalt—almost always indirectly, through his Congressional contacts—on personnel issues, shipyards, ship-building techniques, and any other fault he could find. He was particularly fond of criticizing the US Naval Academy, saying he much preferred university ROTC graduates over those from Annapolis. He said academy graduates were "coddled" through their training and could not handle the academic challenges of the nuclear Navy.

Norman Polmar and Thomas Allen, in their biography, cite Admiral Rickover as "The Unaccountable Man." There is ample evidence that indeed he *was* "unaccountable."

Operating on a near-parallel course, and with the same zeal and crude unconventionality, General LeMay was also "unaccountable." Yet, these two Cold War leaders, who made enemies quicker and fewer than friends, were the geniuses who literally *forced* creation and development of the most powerful war-fighting forces in the history of the world.

Chapter 3

The Weapon Systems

"It was quite a day. The sky was full of B-29s, but I am sure they had a better view of it all from down below than we did. There were two things that struck me at the time. One, of course, was the tremendous, historic event that was taking place beneath us in Tokyo Bay. The other was the amazement at being able to fly around over downtown Tokyo at 1,000 feet altitude and not have anyone shooting at us." These were the thoughts of Lt Gen James V. Edmundson, USAF, Retired, on 2 September 1945, then a colonel and commander of the 468th Bomb Group, as he led five hundred B-29s in a flyover of the Japanese surrender ceremonies aboard the USS *Missouri.* A few weeks later, the 468th and the other groups of the 58th Bomb Wing returned from the Pacific Theater to Sacramento, California, where they were told they would be separated from the Air Corps immediately: "Just sign these papers and you are free to go home. The war is over!"

They were also told that their airplanes would eventually be dismantled and scrapped by waiting contractors. As we know, however, saner judgments prevailed and the initial chaos of demobilizing and dismantling the military services did not commence with the haste that the bureaucrats and "bean counters" may have desired. Fortunately so! One war *was* over, but another had already begun.

Only six months after the 468th flyover, the Secretary of War directed the Army Air Corps to establish the Strategic Air Command (SAC). The order came in response to the growing realization that Stalin's postwar goals went beyond Russia and Eastern Europe. The SAC mandate was to build an organization for long-range offensive operations to any part of the world. SAC began with approximately 100,000 personnel, mostly volunteers who wanted to remain in the Air Corps, and 1,300 various airplanes.

The conglomerate of aircraft consisted of B-29s, P-51 fighters, F-2 and F-13 reconnaissance planes, and a few C-54 transports. But the hastily begun postwar demobilization process couldn't be promptly stemmed, and SAC's manpower eventually dropped to a little over 37,000 by the end of the year. Those who remained were the *committed* and the *dedicated;* they inaugurated SAC. A program to recover airplanes from the war zones continued, and the B-29 fleet grew to over five hundred. The Air Force still lacked mission coherency, however, and SAC's aircraft inventory had grown by 1947 to an odd mixture of 230 P-51s and 120 P-80s for fighter escort duty along with an array of RB-17s, F-2s, F-82s, and RC-45s for reconnaissance missions. These modest reconnaissance aircraft were to be a blessing in disguise, setting the stage for SAC to become the long-term single manager of air-breathing reconnaissance platforms. They were directly related to SAC's strategic mission planning and, later, to the comprehensive intelligence requirements of the future Joint Strategic Target Planning Staff (JSTPS). By 1948, SAC had kicked into high gear and a dramatic evolution in strategic warfare capability had begun.

The Bomber

B-29 *Superfortress.* Developed by Boeing during the war years, the B-29 gave the United States a "long-rifle" capability that the B-17 and B-24 did not have. The heavy bomber concept was consistent with American military thought from the earliest of air war-fighting developments—"fight the war on the other guy's turf whenever possible." Gen William "Billy" Mitchell had long argued that bombers could fly far out to sea and sink the enemy's ships or drop bombs on his capitals, a situation which would be far better than fighting the war in our own territory.

The bomber evolution was slow between the two world wars as several US aircraft companies—Boeing, Martin, Curtiss, Douglas, Lockheed, Consolidated Vultee (Convair)—attempted to develop the desired long-range bomber. The Air Corps had requested a bomber that could fly at speeds of 300 MPH, with a range of 3,000 miles and at an altitude of 35,000 feet. All too often, however, the contractor tried to sell the Air Corps what it thought it needed rather than what was asked for.

World War II brought the issue to a preliminary conclusion. While the Boeing B-17, first of the US heavy bombers, did not entirely fulfill the long-range military strategists' desires to "fly missions from the US mainland to foreign targets," it became the most famous bomber of the day. At the end of the war, 12,731 Flying Fortresses had been built. The B-17 was not the production leader, however; Consolidated Vultee/Convair built over 18,000 B-24 Liberators—more than any other aircraft before or since.

Meanwhile, Boeing had begun back in 1940 to design a "super" bomber—the XB-29. The aircraft's designers attempted to fully address the long-rifle bombing concept. The thinking was that European bases might not always be available to the United States. The XB-29 was dubbed the "Hemisphere Defense Weapon." In designing it, Boeing looked ahead to the potential for the basic structural innovations of the B-29 to be applicable to the all-jet bombers of the future.

Other ideas under consideration were turbojet and pusher engines. The war was ongoing, however, and the "super" aircraft had to be completed as soon as possible—which it was. The first B-29 prototype flew in 1942, two years after the initial design, and the first production models came off the line in 1944. The new strategic bomber had the first pressurized crew compartment and was powered by four 2200-horsepower R-3350 Wright Cyclone engines. The aircraft was fitted with remotely controlled gun turrets, the APQ-7 radar bombing system, double bomb bays, and an engine central fire control system. It also had the size and power to carry large weapons, such as the atomic bomb; the Air Corps ordered 1,660 B-29s. The aircraft's achievements in Europe and the Pacific Theater, including the bombings of Japan, set the stage for strategic bombers of the future. As a demonstration of the newly organized SACs capability, 101 B-29s flew in the command's first "Max-Effort" mission launched on 16 May 1947, flying an extended navigation route and a simulated bomb run on New York City. SAC later had 187 B-29 bombers converted to airborne tankers—KB-29s—and more than 60 to reconnaissance platforms—RB-29s. Earlier versions of the KB-29 were fitted with the British-developed in-flight refueling system, which used trailing hoses and grapnel hooks. Later, in 1950, the KB-29s were fitted with the telescoping "stiff boom" system. The Soviets, equally impressed with the large bomber, built a thousand unauthorized replicas—the TU-4. Some of the B/RB/KB-29s remained in the SAC inventory until 1956; the TU-4 remained in the Soviet inventory well into the 1960s.

B-50A *Advanced Superfortress.* The B-50A was an enhanced version of the B-29, with more reliable Pratt & Whitney R-4360 3500-horsepower engines. The first B-50A aircraft was delivered to SAC on 20 February 1948. Over 250 of the newer bombers, equipped with an engine analyzer to diagnose engine problems and outfitted with a taller vertical stabilizer for improved maneuverability, were built. While the B-50A had a range of 4,900 miles (unrefueled) and an operational altitude of 36,000 feet, it had an air-refueling capability and was also configured as a long-range reconnaissance platform. The last B-50 was phased out of the active inventory on 20 October 1955.

B-36 *Peacemaker.* The B-36 holds perhaps the most unique place in military aviation history. The largest bomber ever built, it could fly in excess of 10,000 miles, unrefueled and carrying a 10,000-pound payload. The Army Air Corps announced the design competition for the bomber on 11 April 1941, eight months before Pearl Harbor and five years before the atomic bomb. In addition to its weight and range capabilities, the Air Corps wanted it to have an airspeed of 300 to 400 MPH and an operating capability from 5,000-foot runways. Convair of San Diego won the contract to build two prototypes to be delivered in 30 months, or about May 1944. Even though the war shifted Convair's priorities to production of the B-24, work continued on building a mock-up of the XB-36. The partially finished mock-up was eventually shipped by rail to a new assembly plant at Fort Worth, Texas. Convair's initial design of the huge bomber called for six Pratt & Whitney Wasp major engines, with 19-foot three-bladed pusher propellers mounted on the trailing edge of the wing. Each 28-cylinder, 4-bank, radial engine had two super-chargers that could produce three thousand horsepower up to an altitude of 35,000 feet. The huge engines in the "pusher" configuration projected a distinctive and unique sound because it was virtually impossible to synchronize all six propellers at the same time with reasonable precision. The result was that the B-36 couldn't "sneak up" on anyone—it sounded like a flight of bass-throated bumblebees about to attack and projecting its noise miles ahead and behind. My wife used to comment that she could begin hanging her wash on the clothesline when a B-36 could be heard coming from high over the horizon, and finish hanging the clothes by the time its "moan" disappeared in the distance. The initial mock-up design of the B-36 was fitted with a twin tail assembly, which was later changed to a single vertical stabilizer. The vertical tail was deemed more stable, but it measured 46 feet, 10 inches from the ground to the top. This latter feature of its large dimensions required special very heavy bomber (VHB) hangars to be built with a padded circular hole in the hanger doors to permit the tall tail to always remain outside. Each wing section had three rubber-coated self-sealing fuel tanks, for a total of six. Together, the six tanks could hold 21,053 gallons of fuel. Outer panel tanks added 2,770 gallons and auxiliary wing tanks added another 9,577 gallons. A bomb bay tank, added later, held approximately three thousand gallons of fuel. The B-36J, the last major modification, had a fuel capacity of 32,965 gallons or roughly 214,273 lbs, which gave the aircraft a takeoff weight of approximately 410,000 lbs.

The wingspan of the bomber from initial design throughout production was maintained at 230 feet, and the fuselage measured 163 feet. An unusual feature was a single wing spar that extended from wing tip to wing tip and supported 90 percent of the engine and wing fuel tank load. The bomber's electrical system operated on a 208/115-volt, 400-cycle alternating current system. DC converters were used to operate instruments and other components requiring direct current power.

The prototype cockpit in the Peacemaker had a much smaller canopy than the final "green house" version that was adopted for the production models. The cockpit was reasonably "roomy," with a wide expanse between the two pilots and an equally wide console to house the six throttles, trim controls, and some radios. The flight engineer's console sat at an angle behind the pilots and contained "all" of the engine operating controls and instruments, electrical power, fuel

35

management systems, and environmental system controls, along with a duplicate set of throttles. The pilots had duplicate manifold pressure gages for use in adjusting power settings for takeoff and landing. The bombardier-navigator compartment was another story—the three members of the bomb-nav team pretty well had to "muscle" for space. If a mission required instructors or evaluators, it was even more crowded. The radio operators, on the other hand, enjoyed a "living room," as did the gunners in the pressurized aft compartment. The B-36D, the 54th production model of the bomber, introduced a jet engine pod under the outer edge of each wing. Each pod contained two J-47 turbojet engines to assist in heavyweight takeoffs and to provide backup power for landings, climbing, and maintaining desired speeds at high altitude. The engine controls for the jet engines were placed above and to the left of the copilot's position. The earlier B-36s were all returned to Convair for addition of the J-47 engines. Both the forward crew compartment and the aft gunner compartment were pressurized. The two compartments were connected by an 85-foot-long, 25-inch diameter, pressurized tube. A small rail-mounted pull cart moved crew members between compartments.

The initial design underwent several major changes throughout the aircraft's development. The landing gear on the first prototype had two large single wheels measuring 110 inches in diameter, which limited the bomber to runways that had a concrete thickness of 22½ inches—and there were only three such military airfields in the United States. But the main problem with the oversized landing gear wheels was the enormous pressure exerted on the gear struts when the plane landed. One of the landing struts collapsed on an early test flight, which drove the development of a four-wheel truck unit that greatly reduced both the landing "footprint" and the stress exerted on the strut. The four-wheel truck configuration required a nominal 300-foot-wide runway to safely accommodate the aircraft's turning radius, although a skilled pilot could maneuver the airplane around with considerably less operating space. After several attempts to meet the Air Force's requirements for armament, Convair outfitted the bomber with an elaborate defensive weapons system consisting of sixteen 20-millimeter (mm) cannons mounted in pairs in eight remotely controlled retractable turrets. The protective armament provided a full 360-degree protection radius while the bomber was in flight. A built-in contour arrangement on the turrets prevented the guns from firing at the tall vertical stabilizer. The standard bomber crew consisted of 15 members: three pilots (aircraft commander, pilot, and copilot), three bombing-navigation specialists (radar bombardier, navigator, co-observer), two flight engineers, two radio/electronic warfare operators, and five gunners. In the forward compartment, the copilot, co-observer, and number two radio operator were trained to operate and fire the remote turrets. Flight crew requirements varied with the aircraft configuration, however. The RB-36D/F/H reconnaissance model, for example, carried a 23-man crew. In this version, the forward bomb bay was enclosed and pressurized for additional equipment and operating space.

The development of the B-36 was not only an engineering challenge; it was a hard-fought battle within and between the services. The Navy set out to discredit strategic airpower in an attempt to get a larger share of the defense budget for its own fleet programs, large carriers in particular. A "well-meaning" Navy "team player" anonymously wrote a document, ostensibly without the knowledge of his superiors, detailing 55 serious accusations against the development of the B-36 and its proponents. The document was traced to the Office of the Secretary of the Navy and, finally, to Cedric R. Worth, an assistant to the Undersecretary of the Navy. Worth finally admitted that he had largely made up the accusations. A lengthy investigation into the possibility that there had been higher-level direction to create and distribute the document ended with Mr. Worth accepting sole blame.

Within a short time, the infamous "Admirals' Revolt" erupted and the B-36 was targeted again. The furor was over money and global priorities. The Air Force, SAC in particular, had won most of the budget battles for strategic systems. In 1958, nine years after this brouhaha, defense budget summaries would reflect that aircraft and missiles had accounted for 58 percent of all DOD expenditures between the start of the Korean War and 1958. A whopping 67 percent had been allocated to the Air Force from 1954 to 1958. The admirals likely had reason to be frustrated and angry, but they simply had not made their strategic case strong enough or soon enough.

Rep. Carl Vinson, chairman of the House Armed Services Committee, called for hearings "to deal with all facts relating to matters involving the B-36 bomber." Vinson, who reputedly had a fondness for the Navy, declared that he would "let the chips fall where they may." He called 35 witnesses, among which were virtually every senior general officer in the Air Force and the leaders of every major aircraft company. General Kenney testified that he had at first favored the B-36. In 1946, after becoming commander of SAC, he became convinced that the bomber was not performing satisfactorily and recommended that production be halted. By 1948, however, a dramatic turnaround had occurred and "It suddenly became evident that we had available in the B-36 the fastest, longest-ranged, best altitude-performing, and heaviest load-carrying plane in the world."

To a man, the Air Force leadership testified that the B-36 was "the heart of any global air striking force." Gen Henry H. "Hap" Arnold was called out of retirement to testify. He chastised the Committee and the detractors of the B-36 for attempting to disrupt the development of an immediate strategic deterrence requirement and for giving away secret performance information in open hearings. Arnold's testimony was powerful and sharp. He gave credit to Generals Kenney and LeMay for their candor and for taking the responsibility to build a believable strategic fighting force while others "whimpered" about what "ought" to be done. Arnold's appearance before the Vinson Committee was his last; he died shortly afterward.

There was an attempt to play the future B-47 against the B-36. LeMay said he would take the B-36 now and take his chances with the unproven jet technology when the time came. Others testifying included Generals Carl A. Spaatz, Hoyt S. Vandenberg, Lauris Norstad, and Nathen Twining, along with the Secretary of the Air Force, W. Stuart Symington; each testified strongly for the B-36.

Finally, the Navy's Mr. Worth was called to testify, under oath, before the Committee. During his testimony, he made a startling revelation—he had been a newspaper reporter and Hollywood script writer before being appointed to the Navy Department. The Navy was embarrassed, Worth was severely censured, and the hearings were concluded. The battle for the B-36 was won.

On 26 June 1948, the first of the largest and heaviest bombers ever built up to that time, the B-36A, was delivered to SAC's 7th Bombardment Wing at Carswell AFB, Texas. By the end of the year, 35 aircraft had been delivered. SAC celebrated the success of the program by staging a long-range navigation and bombing mission that extended from taking off at Carswell through dropping a 10,000-pound "dummy" bomb in the Pacific Ocean near the Hawaiian Islands and returning to Carswell. The unrefueled mission covered 8,100 miles in 35½ hours. The mission was, in a way, a "LeMay triumph" in that the bomber made an approach over Honolulu undetected by the local air defense system—on 7 December 1948!

Early in 1949, another B-36 crew set a long-distance record of 9,600 miles. The B-36 covered the distance in 43 hours, 37 minutes. Recalling these "feats" of aerial accomplishment brought the fond memory of a nonstop flight from Guam to Biggs AFB, Texas, my crew made in 1955. That trip took 34 hours, 40 minutes. There was little doubt that the vast Soviet communications monitoring system was taking note of these and other similar demonstrations of long-range strategic "reach."

There were several follow-on "test" versions and modifications of the B-36. One such version was the "C" model prototype, which had six turboprop engines on the forward edge of the wings; each extended some ten feet from the leading edge. The video display terminal (VDT) turboprops would have boosted the bomber's airspeed to 410 MPH and a service ceiling of 45,000 feet, enhancing its "over the target" dash speed. An initial order of 34 aircraft was canceled when the engine failed to deliver the promised performance. The overall B-36 program followed a precarious path of indecision even after it had won its political battles, budget costs being the persistent enemy. The Soviets, however, in their inimitable way, boosted the bomber program into new life with the Berlin Blockade, prompting Secretary Symington to direct full production of the original contract. Following the retrofitting of all B-36s with the J-47 engines, the B-36F, H, and J configurations came along. These included newer R-4360-53 engines with more power and reliability. The K-3A radar bombing system was added to provide for both precision radar and visual bombing capability. Some of the bomb bay systems were modified to carry the MK-17 thermonuclear bomb, the largest ever developed. It weighed 42,000 lbs and measured 24½ feet in length. The B-36J "Featherweight" modification program reduced the aircraft's weight appreciably by removing all of the 20-mm retractable turrets except the tail gun, thereby reducing the crew requirement (to 13) and by reducing "drag" on the airplane by replacing the large gunner's blisters with flush windows or plugs. The "J" model had an increased range, higher speed (418 MPH at 37,500 ft), and a service ceiling of 43,600 feet. The FICON (Fighter-Conveyor) modification was made on 11 aircraft assigned to the 99th Strategic Recon Wing at Fairchild AFB, near Spokane, Washington. Designated the GRB-36D/F, these bombers were modified to carry and retrieve the F-84E and, later, the RF-84K reconnaissance-fighter aircraft as an extension of the RB-36's reconnaissance capability. The GRB-36 could take off with the RF-84K "tucked" in its bomb bay, fly a nominal radius of 2,810 miles and launch the "parasite" fighter at 25,000 feet. The RF-84K, carrying five cameras and four 50-caliber guns, weighed 29,500 lbs at release.

The tactic added approximately 1,100 miles to the reconnaissance-fighter's radius of flight. It could fly to a target area, take pictures, and dash back to the "mother ship." In late 1955, after 170 successful launches and retrievals, the unit was declared combat-ready with 10 GRB-36s and 25 RF-84Ks. After a year, however, the program was suddenly canceled. A similar pilot program, called Tom-Tom, featured modified RB-36s and RF-84Ks mated with a wing-tip launch and retrieval system. The program proved workable, but with considerable risk and fatigue on the part of both aircraft.

Convair developed the prototype YB-60, an eight-jet, swept-wing version of the B-36. Its performance was a quantum leap over the B-36, but it did not compete favorably with the performance of the prototype B-52. Convair also "toyed with" developing a nuclear-powered version of the B-36—the NB-36H. It did not use nuclear power, but it carried an onboard nuclear reactor to test radiation shielding and the potential effects of radiation on the crew and the aircraft. The cumbersome 12-inch-thick cockpit window glass, and the closed-circuit television system designed to monitor the engines, proved too costly, cumbersome, and inefficient. After 47 flights, the program was canceled.

Lastly, a large-body passenger-cargo version of the B-36 configuration—the XC-99—was flown in 1947. Its oversized fuselage could carry four hundred combat troops or 50 tons of cargo. Only one XC-99 was built, but it was used extensively during the Korean War to haul cargo back and forth across the United States. After the war, it continued to operate under Military Air Transport Service (MATS) until 1957. The XC-99 was retired to its permanent "pedestal" at Kelly AFB, near San Antonio, Texas. Pan American Airways had placed an option order to buy three C-99s for their Hawaii route, but canceled it when they determined that there was insufficient passenger traffic to support the aircraft's large capacity.

Maintaining and flying the B-36 took on a life of its own for the maintenance teams and combat crews associated with the complex bomber. While it was relatively easy and straight-forward to fly, and incredibly "forgiving" of human errors, it nevertheless required an inordinate amount of maintenance, care, and preparation to operate. The maintenance crew chief and team were required to be fully coordinated with the flight crew. The aircraft status and maintenance information "hand-off" from ground to flight crew was essential. The complex electrical, hydraulic, fuel, engine, avionics, communications, and flight control systems required that flight crew members be expertly knowledgeable in their operation. Consequently, B-36 combat crews tended to be highly stable with minimal crew changes over extended periods of time—often years. Crew coordination was critical to the success of every mission. Like the long flights, operational preflight by the combat crew was also long and extensive. Preflight began four hours before the scheduled takeoff time. The pilots conducted their routine checks: walkaround, struts, tire inflation, fuel and oil leaks, propellers for nicks, control surfaces, and general condition. The flight engineers had by far the most comprehensive preflight checks, allowing little time for weather interference or maintenance problems. They had to crawl into the wings and check for fuel and oil leaks and any signs of engine or flight control problems. Severe weather only added to the difficulty of their task. They also climbed into the cavernous wheel wells to check all of the control linkages and hydraulic lines. The copilot (3d pilot) was tasked to measure (dip-stick) all the fuel tanks against the planned fuel load for the mission. Since this was accomplished from the top of the wing, weather conditions could make it a "sporty" exercise. The remainder of the crew conducted their respective systems checks, ranging from routine to very complex; when practice bombs were to be dropped or the guns were to be practice-fired, then considerable detail had to be given to those systems. Engine start was initiated 45 minutes before the scheduled takeoff time. (Today's jet aircraft would already be airborne and at altitude.)

Taxiing and steering the huge "monster" was relatively easy, the main concern being wing tip clearance for moving through other aircraft. The pilots had excellent visibility, but sat approximately 70 feet in front of the main gear, making it necessary to constantly ensure that the area 180 degrees around and at least 250 feet wide was clear to move the "beast." Takeoffs in the B-36 were extremely pleasant and smooth. The power of the six pusher engines and the four jets provided all the thrust necessary to launch the airplane at any gross weight. For its size, it also handled extremely well in turns and during climb-out; its control pressures were exceptionally light. Likewise, both approach and landing were very straightforward and fun—*under most conditions!* Cross-winds constituted the obvious exception, given the B-36's wide wing spread and tall tail. The final approach was usually at about 125 MPH, with touchdown at 100 MPH for a smooth landing. Even with the cockpit "floating" at 40 feet above the ground at touchdown, visibility and control were excellent. Thunderstorms, a "few" engines out, or a fire, however, created an entirely different environment. No pilot or crew member who ever served aboard the mighty ten-engine aircraft had anything but respect for her capability and safety—but mainly for the unique pleasure of flying with her.

For further reading, the B-36 enthusiast should read *Peacemaker: History of the B-36* (Prologue by Lt Gen Harry Goldsworthy); *Six Churning and Four Burning*, a three-part series "reflection" by Gen James V. ("Jim") Edmundson; and *B-36 in Action*, by Meyers K. Jacobsen and Ray Wagner. The words quoted here are those of Gen James V. Goldsworthy.

> The public relations people dubbed the B-36, this gentle giant, the *Peacemaker*, a name that never caught on with the crews, and it droned through the skies of the world until February 1959 without dropping a bomb or firing a shot in anger. The jet age left the aircraft obsolete after a relatively short life span, and when it was flown to the boneyard, it was the end of a proud era of heavy bombers powered by reciprocating engines. Technology passed it by and left it out-performed, but never out-classed. The B-36 wasn't an agile bird—in fact, at times it could be downright ponderous—but it was honest. Crews had confidence that it would get there and bring them home. It was modified and abused, always pressed to come up with more performance. And it seemed to respond with more than anyone had the right to expect. If its crews did not always love it, they surely respected it. And perhaps the *Peacemaker* wasn't so bad after all. We will never know what the course of world events would have been without the B-36 standing ready to deliver its awesome load to any point in the world in a few short hours.

The B-36 never dropped a bomb in combat during its ten years of active duty, but it remained ready and capable; SAC owned over 150 B/RB-36s by the end of 1950. However, the bomber was held out of the Korean War as it continued to perform its nuclear deterrent role. In August and September 1953, after the Korean truce, SAC sent a flight of B-36s to the Far East, landing airplanes in Japan, Okinawa, and Guam to demonstrate US resolve to back peace in the region.

A total of 385 B-36s of various models and configurations were delivered to the Air Force. The last B-36, a "J" model Featherweight, was retired from the 95th Bomb Wing, Biggs AFB, Texas, on 12 February 1959. Its final flight was made to Fort Worth, Texas, to be placed on permanent display. A few others were given to airports and museums around the country. The best-preserved B-36 resides comfortably, in "mint condition," *inside* the Air Force Museum at Wright-Patterson AFB, Ohio.

B-47 *Stratojet.* The Army Air Corps initiated a request in 1943 for the aircraft industry to study the feasibility of an all-jet bomber. The Germans had already begun work on jet propulsion engines (they were flying a jet fighter-bomber before World War II ended) and the British were far ahead of the Americans in developing jet fighter and bomber prototypes. In 1944, the Air Corps called for a bomber aircraft that would fly at least 500 MPH. Five manufacturers promptly submitted preliminary designs. North American offered the XB-45, which in the end became the first all-jet bomber to go into production. It operated successfully as a light bomber and reconnaissance aircraft in Korea and through the 1950s. Convair, which presented the most competitive bomber, was not considered because it had won the B-24 and B-36 contracts (the "wealth" had to be "spread around"). Martin and Northrop offered acceptable designs, but their aircraft were not large enough to perform truly strategic bombing missions. Northrop's "flying wing" design was determined to be too radical. (It showed up again in the 1990s as the B-2.)

Boeing won the competition with its XB-47, a six-engine aircraft having a swept-wing design and a bicycle landing gear configuration. Boeing engineers leaned heavily on their B-29 design concepts, although the B-29 had little in common, physically, with the B-47. However, the stressed webbed-wing design, landing gear struts, low-pressure hydraulic system, and 28-volt DC electrical system found places in the B-47 design. The early major shortfall in the bomber was the low technology of its jet engines. The excessively long "spool-up" time on the initial J-35 engine was critical in landing situations. And the total thrust of the six J-35s was rated at only 21,500 lbs for the planned 125,000-lb aircraft. Consequently, carrying high power on approaches mandated landing at higher than desired speed and with longer roll-out. A drag chute to offset the high power settings during approach, and a brake chute to slow the aircraft after touchdown, were added. An antiskid brake system provided an additional safety factor. As development proceeded, J-47 GE engines, each having 5,200 lbs of thrust, replaced the underpowered J-35. The bomber began to look more practical to the designer and to the Air Force. The final design gave the bomber a 107-foot fuselage and a 116-foot wingspan. The wing had an extraordinary flexible deflection of 17½ feet, tip-to-tip. The bicycle landing gear was chosen because the thin wings couldn't accommodate wheel wells. The gear was retracted into the fuselage section.

The three crew members—pilot, copilot, radar-navigator—were "tucked" into a small, pressurized cabin compartment, minimizing the need for a large pressurization and environmental system. In September 1948, the Air Force placed an order for ten B-47As for capabilities testing. The aircraft were assembled at Boeing's facility in Wichita, Kansas, adjacent to McConnell AFB where the first Air Force B-47 crew training would eventually take place. This concept had proven successful with the Convair B-36 assembly facility collocated with the first recipient unit, the 7th Bomb Wing, at Carswell AFB, Texas. The B-47's refueling capability was initially supported by the KC-97 "Stratotanker" and later by the KC-135 (a Boeing 707). "Fly Away" kits were designed and built, allowing the B-47 to deploy anywhere in the world, carrying along spare parts and equipment. The B-47 filled a large gap in the US strategic inventory and gave war planners broad flexibility in covering the Soviet target complex. SAC would eventually reach a peak of 1,367 B-47s and an additional 176 RB-47 reconnaissance aircraft.

The B-47, not unlike virtually all military weapons systems, was designed for one principal mission; and not unlike virtually all military weapons systems, it was employed in other, sometimes radical, ways to meet new threats. In order to attain greater distances with heavier payloads, the gross weight of the aircraft grew from the original 125,000 lbs to 230,000 lbs for taxi and takeoff, with a maximum in-flight weight of 226,000 lbs. These additional requirements placed considerable stress and fatigue on the airframe, shortening its life span. Additional strain was placed on the aircraft with the introduction of "pop-up" maneuvers designed to avoid Soviet antiaircraft missiles along single integrated operation plan (SIOP) routes and target areas.

In the "pop-up" maneuver, the B-47 flew into a defended area at 300-500 feet altitude and at high speed. The aircraft then climbed rapidly to about 18,000 feet, dropped a nuclear weapon on the target, made a sharp turn, and descended back down to treetop altitude. This maneuver enabled the bomber to avoid the blast effects from the released bomb.

In a similar maneuver Low Altitude Bombing System (LABS), the aircraft flew into the target area at low altitude and high speed but pulled up into a half loop just prior to the bomb release point. The pilot then released the bomb, and rolled the aircraft out in an "Immelmann" maneuver to avoid the impact of the nuclear explosion.

Neither large bombers nor bomber pilots were well suited for these fighter-type aerobatics. They subjected the airplane to potentially severe "g" forces, inducing even further fatigue. SAC reported six B-47 crashes in a one-month period during the Spring of 1958, all attributed to wear and fatigue in wing skins and fuselage fittings.

Maj Gen Earl G. Peck, former SAC Chief of Staff, and a B-47 aircraft commander as a young Air Force captain, described the experience of flying the B-47:

The Boeing B-47, officially the "Stratojet," was one of those airplanes that never seemed to acquire any sort of affectionate nickname. This probably stems from the fact that although it was often admired, respected, cursed, or even feared, it was almost never loved. In fact, I think it would be fair to say that it tended to separate the "men" from the "boys!" It was relatively difficult to land, terribly unforgiving of mistakes or inattention, subject to control reversal at high speeds, and suffered from horrible roll-due-to-yaw characteristics. Cross-wind landings and takeoffs were sporty, and in-flight discrepancies were the rule rather than exception. All in all, the B-47 was a very demanding machine for her three-man crew. But, its idiosyncrasies notwithstanding, the B-47 served as a mainstay of the SAC deterrent posture during the darkest years of the protracted Cold War. Thus a typical B-47 mission was comprised of all those activities that the crew had to master if the system was to serve as a credible deterrent. They were also the same things that would be required during a nuclear strike mission if deterrence failed: high- and low-level navigation and weapon delivery, aerial refueling, electronic countermeasures against air and ground threats, positive control procedures, exercising the tail-mounted 20-mm guns, emergency procedures, cell (formation) tactics, and others I am sure I have forgotten. Crew planning for a mission took up *most of the day prior* and was elaborately precise and detailed. The crew was expected to approach each training sortie with the same meticulous professionalism that would be required for an actual strike mission. And professionalism keynoted the mission attitude that prevailed from inception to completion. On the day of the flight, [there were] an exhaustive series of inspections—station, exterior, and interior...perusal of forms, equipment, and safety items...walkaround inspection of aircraft...system-by-system interior inspection. Finally finding the bird fit, we would leave it and wend our way to base ops for a weather briefing and to compute takeoff data and file a clearance. Taxiing the B-47 was relatively easy. Takeoff in a B-47 was, to my knowledge, unique in its day, for the airplane in effect was "flying" shortly after beginning the roll. This could be attributed to the flexible wings, which permitted the outriggers to lift off as soon as the airflow generated any appreciable lift. Somewhat ungainly on the ground, the B-47 assumed a classic grace in flight. Aerial refueling presented its own difficulties, stemming principally from incompatibility with the piston-driven KC-97 tankers then in use. Very-high-wing loading and associated stall speeds in the B-47 meant that the KC-97 was taxed to provide any respectable margin above stall while hooked up. [The KC-97 more often than not had to maintain a continuous descent during air refueling with the B-47 and the B-52 in order for the heavy bombers to maintain sufficient airspeed to avoid stalling out]. On one particularly dark night, in fact, my airplane stalled off the boom and fluttered gracefully down 5,000 feet of murk before it became a flying machine again! Looking back, although much of the flying I did in the B-47 was not particularly enjoyable—it was in fact tedious, demanding, even grueling at times—it was terribly rewarding in terms of professional satisfaction. I felt I was doing an important job and took great pride in doing it well in a machine capable of performing. As with most airplanes, the advertised performance figures (4,000 nautical-mile range, 600 MPH speed, 40,000 feet service ceiling) didn't mean much to the guys flying the B-47. It was only important that it would go fast and far enough to enable a group of professional, dedicated and gutsy SAC crews to provide the bulk of American deterrent strength during the middle and late 1950s. As the decade waned, the B-47 was gradually supplemented and later supplanted by the B-52 as SAC's "big stick"; but the "Stratojet" had written an important chapter in military history.

B-52 *Stratofortress*. The B-47 created a success story for Boeing and big bombers. Walter Boyne, author of *Boeing B-52, A Documentary History,* credited Boeing's bold vision and several young Air Force officers (who were not overly inhibited by the existing bureaucracy) with the key decisions that led to the development of the B-52. "Similarly," he said, "senior officers were still permitted to exercise the vision, imagination, and leadership which were then and are still the primary reasons for their existence." A careful review of bomber histories, particularly the B-70, B-58, B-1, and, to some extent the FB-111, confirms Boyne's assessment to a large extent. The B-2 may become a victim of the same syndrome of too many experts, too many built-in requirements, and too many politicians. "The Congress, in its desire to know everything about a weapon system in real time, has put itself in the position of a restaurant customer checking in with the chef every step of the way, sampling, tasting, directing, changing his mind, and making decisions long before the menu is defined."

In 1946, Boeing was finishing off the B-29, had a few orders for the B-50, and was concentrating on the first true all-jet strategic bomber, the B-47. The Army Air Corps, anticipating the demise over time of the large reciprocating engine and the "experimental" XB-36, placed a requirement on the aviation industry for a "second generation" heavy bomber. Boeing engineers, however, could not produce a design that exceeded the B-36. The main shortfall was in turbojet engine technology. The B-47 had experienced the same problem in its initial development—insufficient power to fly the airplane at the desired gross weights. Finally, Pratt & Whitney agreed to build the largest jet engine they possibly could. The J-57 would be a quantum leap above the J-47, and would initially produce 10,000 lbs of thrust. The production model B-52B engines would be improved to produce 12,100 lbs thrust each, and eventually the "F" model J-57 would be rated at 13,750 lbs of thrust.

Convair attempted to meet the heavy jet bomber requirement with its jet-powered YB-36, but fell short. Boeing, however, presented a proposal for an eight-jet aircraft built along the lines of the B-47. This bomber would be much larger, having a gross weight of roughly 330,000 lbs, an eight-thousand-mile range carrying a 10,000-lb bomb, and a cruising speed of 570 MPH. The first prototype rolled out in November 1951. An ecstatic General LeMay went to work to get the necessary funding to produce the bomber. He also directed changes in the design; specifically, he did not like the B-47-type tandem seating for the pilots. Boeing therefore changed the cockpit to a side-by-side configuration for better crew coordination. Soon after flight tests began to show progress, LeMay directed that range and gross weight be increased. The later "G" and "H" models eventually reached takeoff gross weights of 488,000 lbs, and the B-52H would be powered by a state-of-the-art TF33-P-3 engine having a flat-rated thrust of 17,000 lbs.

The first production B-52 was the "B" model, delivered to SAC on 29 June 1955. It was indeed a large jet aircraft, with a 185-foot wingspan and a fuselage measuring 140 feet in length. The bomb bay, measuring 28 feet by 6 feet, could accommodate any of the nuclear weapons in the inventory. The flexible wing, similar in design to the B-47, has an incredible deflection of 32 feet! This feature was at first very disconcerting to the pilots when they glanced back at the wings during considerable turbulence (the wings would be slowly flapping). The top of the original tail section was 48 feet from the ground. In the first B-52s, the two pilots were seated in the upper cockpit with the navigator and radar-navigator (bombardier) directly below them. The electromagnetic countermeasures officer (ECM), later renamed the electronic warfare officer (EWO), sat behind the pilots at the rear of the pressurized compartment. The tail gunner was tightly fitted in a pressurized compartment located in the rearmost end of the fuselage tail section. The tail gunner's *was not* a happy position—particularly due to the cramped quarters, but also because of the bomber's twisting movement and "see-saw" motions even in the lightest of turbulence. Egress by the tail gunner from the aircraft in an emergency also presented a special problem: He had to pull an ejection handle to remove the tail section, then manually bail out. This would normally work if the aircraft had not rolled into a nose-down dive, in which case he could have difficulty in overcoming the 'g' forces enough to pull himself out. Air sickness was common and morale amongst tail gunners was terrible—yet, amazingly, they flew on! Later, in the "G" and "H" models, the gunner was moved to the forward pressurized compartment and positioned in an ejection seat side-by-side with the EWO. There, the tail gunner became a "happy camper." The earlier bombers were equipped with four 50-caliber machine guns in the tail. The later "H" model was fitted with a six-barrel M-61 20-mm Gatling gun. The fire control system, with either gun configuration, has the capability to search, detect, acquire, track, and compute the angle of attack of an incoming aircraft. The gunner also is equipped with a periscope gunsight for manual aiming and firing; in the "G" and "H" models, he has a rear-projection television monitor. The original B-52 bombing-navigation system was a rudimentary radar tracking and plotting device with a visual optics backup.

Modifications and enhancements, however, have kept the B-52 current with state-of-the-art technology. The MA-6A serves as the bomber's baseline bomb-nav system. The later B-52G and H models were equipped with an Electro-optical Viewing System (EVS)—forward-looking infrared (FLIR) and low-light-level TV sensors integrated into bombing, navigation, and pilot directional systems. Like the B-47, the B-52 is equipped with a bicycle landing gear; but the B-52 version is considerably more complex. The "quadricycle" landing gear, which consists of four wheels in front and four in rear, retracts into the fuselage. The front wheels are steerable for taxi and takeoff, and both front and rear can be canted on final approach to accommodate a crosswind. The pilot can then land the aircraft in a "crabbed" position, touching down with the aircraft at an angle to the centerline of the runway. It takes some getting used to, but it works.

The electrical system consists of four gear-driven constant-speed generators providing 200/115-volt AC power and transformer rectifiers for DC requirements. The B-52 was initially outfitted with 1,000-gallon wingtip fuel tanks; later, with three-thousand-gallon tanks. The tanks provided wing stability as well as additional fuel. The later "G" and "H" models were equipped with smaller 700-gallon tanks, mainly for wing stability. Within two years of first delivery, three B-52s flew nonstop around the world—24,235 miles—in 45 hours and 19 minutes. With Maj Gen Archie Olds, commander of 15th Air Force, in the lead aircraft, the B-52s took off from Castle AFB, California, on 16 January 1957. They landed at March AFB, California, within two minutes of their original planned ETA, with all 24 engines of the three aircraft still running smoothly and only one inoperative alternator on one of the planes.

The B-52G and H models, virtually "new" airplanes, were "luxurious" compared to the 449 "B" through "F" model predecessors. They were some 15,000 lbs (dry weight) lighter, but the aircraft's gross weight was increased to 488,000 lbs.

The fuel was stored in a "wet wing," rather than the now discarded rubberized fuel cells. Fuel capacity was increased to over 310,000 lbs. Ailerons were removed, and lateral control was shifted to the wing spoilers. Crew comfort was enhanced by the addition of more comfortable seats and an improved air conditioning system. The EWO position was upgraded with more sophisticated tracking and jamming systems. The pilots were initially given the advanced capability radar (ACR), which provided terrain avoidance, antijamming, and enhanced low-level mapping capabilities. The ACR system employed small (5-inch) television monitors at each pilot's position and at the navigator's station. The ACR was followed shortly by the EVS, which generated greater confidence and provided greater comfort for a night-weather, low-level flying mission.

All of the B-52 systems underwent constant upgrades and major modifications to keep up with potential enemy threats and evolving technologies. The "H" model B-52 had little resemblance to the first production aircraft, except in overall profile appearance. And even that changed when the vertical stabilizer was shortened to 40 feet on the "G" and "H" models as a growing array of radar and sensor antennas began to "crop-up" around the outer fuselage surfaces. The B-52 has accommodated an ever-increasing volume of weapon systems:

— entire inventory of free-fall and chute-retarded nuclear bombs;

— GAM-72 Quail missile decoy (which with its 13-ft length and 5-ft wingspan replicated the image of a B-52 to an enemy radar);

— GAM-77/AGM-28 Hound Dog air-launched attack missile, one carried under each wing of the Gs and Hs, and equipped with a nuclear warhead;

— GAM-87 Skybolt nuclear warhead air-launched ballistic missile, also carried and launched from under the wing;

— AGM-69A short-range attack missile (SRAM) air-launched missile, up to 20 carried under the wings and in the bomb bay;

— air-breathing turbojet air-launched cruise missile (ALCM), launched from under the wing and from the bomb bay.

51

And the bomber had the incredible capability to carry 108 five-hundred-pound conventional bombs, which it did routinely in Vietnam. The last of 744 B-52s was an "H" model, Serial Number 61-040, delivered on 26 October 1962—*thirty-seven years ago* at the time of this writing. And many of them are still flying! I vividly remember the thrill of my crew traveling from Ramey AFB, Puerto Rico, to the Boeing plant in Wichita, Kansas, in the Fall of 1959 to take delivery of a "brand-spanking new" B-52G bomber and flying it back home. It had the same feeling as picking up a new car at the dealership. It even *smelled* new! That was a whopping *forty* years ago! So it is no wonder that many *sons of fathers* before them have flown and are still flying the mighty B-52. Unlike its SAC predecessors, the B-36 and B-47, both of which were held out of combat, the B-52 performed in Vietnam—and performed well.

The initial unit cost of the B-52A was astronomical—$29.3 million each for the three that were built. However, because the aircraft provided such promise, the decision was made to proceed with development and production. By the time the first "B" models came off the line, the cost of the aircraft had dropped to $14.4 million each, and the B-52E eventually cost $5.9 million per aircraft. The last of the B-52 series, the "H" model, was priced a bit higher—$9.2 million—due to extensive rework and advanced technologies. Undeniably, the B-52 remains the longest *living* bomber in US military aviation history.

Taxiing a fully loaded B-52G out onto the runway, setting the brakes, and pushing the throttles forward to full power for takeoff had a feeling of exhilaration like no other. I am sure fighter pilots experience the same feeling, but for a *much shorter* time. Flying the reliable B-36 had its special feeling of power, mass, and control; but the B-52 had it *all*—and speed to go with it. It was easy to taxi at all gross weights, directional control during takeoff was excellent, and climb-out was very straightforward and smooth. Landing in a crosswind could be "sporty," due to the tall vertical stabilizer (either 40 or 48 feet); but the crosswind landing gear feature, once taken into confidence, compensated very well. Flying at high altitude was a routine procedure, with the exception of large air refueling operations, which required a determined skill. The

24-hour Chromedome sorties required taking on approximately 110,000 lbs of fuel—an operation that demanded 20 to 30 minutes of *sheer flying skill and determination.* At relatively light gross weights and high altitude (30,000 to 35,000 feet), the airplane tended to "float" through the air; a small power adjustment while you were approaching and connecting with the KC-135 tanker would move you about rapidly.

Once the fuel began to fill the wings and the aircraft took on more weight, it became very controllable—except in turbulence, of course! Turbulence required another feat of skill to manage the "flapping wings." Flying the B-52 at extremely low levels—which the B-52 was not originally designed to do—placed the pilots and crew into another challenging dimension. Dropping from 35,000 feet to 500 feet—300 feet on some routes—at night, and maintaining that flying environment for several hundred miles required every ounce of confidence in the airplane and faith in its flight and navigation instruments that one could muster. I flew the B-52 *before* ACR and EVS, so "head and eyeballs" were mostly out of the cockpit while we cross-checked the altimeter as we roared across the federal aviation administration (FAA) approved (and traffic clear?) routes of the US countryside. Importantly, the six crew members were fully integrated into the B-52's weapon system.

There was hardly a minute during a tightly planned and coordinated 14- or 20-hour training mission when the majority of the crew were not interacting with each other. High-altitude navigation, low-level navigation, bomb runs, air refueling, electromagnetic countermeasure testing against simulated radar sites, gunnery practice, fighter intercepts—each activity required attentive concentration. Consequently, "wagging home" the carefully prepared (but undisturbed) flight lunch box which had been delivered fresh to the aircraft by the in-flight kitchen just before takeoff was the norm rather than the exception. (The kids were always delighted to see what marvels of "goodies" [and soggy sandwiches] dad had brought back.)

B-58 *Hustler.* If the B-52 is the oldest and longest living bomber in US military history, the B-58 had one of the shortest "active duty" tours—and fewer than one hundred production aircraft rolled off the assembly line. But it was the only supersonic strategic bomber to enter the Western world's operational inventory. As B-36 production at the General Dynamics Convair facility at Fort Worth came to a halt, the company offered a competitive proposal to develop and build a supersonic medium bomber as a "gap filler" for the anticipated phaseout of the B-47. The Air Force and SAC accepted the proposal, and the first B-58 was delivered at Carswell AFB, Texas, on 1 August 1960. The relatively *small* bomber, 96.8 feet in length with a 56.8-foot wingspan, was powered by four J-79-5A engines, each producing 10,000 lbs of flat-rated thrust—15,600 lbs in afterburner. The pilot, navigator, and defensive systems operator (DSO) were positioned in separate tandem cockpits that were in fact encapsulated seats for ejection. The bomber was *"all airplane"*; it carried a 62-foot-long pod—which had the appearance of an afterthought—beneath its underside to accommodate a nuclear weapon and additional fuel. To safeguard against a blowout or a flat tire causing the aircraft to crush the pod, the landing gear included smaller steel wheels inset between the sets of tires.

The B-58 also suffered from other problems, including one that required the pilot to continuously transfer fuel during taxiing to prevent the airplane from tipping on its tail. Another required the installation of water-filled cooling tanks through which fuel and hydraulic oil were routed to prevent evaporation caused by the extraordinary heat generated within the plane at high speeds. General LeMay was never really satisfied with the B-58; it required an extraordinary number of in-flight refuelings to complete a mission, and it severely taxed a disproportionate share of other SAC resources to maintain its combat readiness. And, as one story had it, LeMay flew the bomber, declared that it was too small and added, "it didn't fit my 'arse'."

As a high-speed aircraft, and for its size, the B-58 was a state-of-the-art product. It broke record after record over the course of its life. Only five months after SAC took delivery, a B-58 established six international speed and payload records, all in a single flight, on 12 January 1961. Pilot Maj Henry J. Deutschendorf, navigator Maj William L. Polhemus, and DSO Capt Raymond R. Wagner, flying out of Edwards AFB without a payload, averaged 1,200 MPH in two laps over a 1,243-mile course. The same crew and aircraft proceeded to fly five additional speed patterns with varying load configurations averaging between 1,200 MPH and 1,061 MPH. Incidentally, Major Deutschendorf, now deceased, was the father of folk singer John Denver.

A B-58 piloted by Maj Elmer E. Murphy set a sustained speed record of 1,302 MPH on 10 May 1961. Less than a month later, however, tragedy struck Major Murphy and his crew when their bomber crashed during a 3 June demonstration flight at the Paris Air Show; all three crew members were killed.

On 26 May 1961, a B-58 piloted by Maj William Payne flew nonstop from New York to Paris—4,612 miles—in 3 hours, 19 minutes, 41 seconds. On 16 October 1963, Maj Henry Kubesch and his crew from the 305th Bomb Wing flew nonstop from Tokyo to London—8,028 miles—in 8 hours, 35 minutes, 20 seconds. Five aerial refuelings were required to complete the mission. In all, the B-58 set 15 world records for speed and altitude. Its achievements include winning the Bendix, Bleriot, Harmon, Mackey, and Thompson trophies. Meanwhile, the B-58 bomber and crew force remained combat-ready, performing training missions and remaining alert as a part of the 43d Bombardment Wing at Carswell AFB, Texas, and the 305th Bombardment Wing at Bunker Hill (later named Grissom) AFB, Indiana. Later B-58s were modified to carry high-resolution cameras in the nose of the pod for performing a reconnaissance role.

SAC reached a peak of 94 assigned B-58s in 1964, just one year before the Johnson Administration directed phaseout of the aircraft. Having had a record-breaking career, the last B-58 was retired on 16 January 1970.

FB-111A *Aardvark.* This "fighter-bomber," initially the F-111 with an unlikely nickname, became an equally unlikely addition to the strategic nuclear force. The FB-111A, a relatively small two-man bomber version of the swing-wing F-111 fighter, was built by General Dynamics at its Fort Worth facility. The two-man side-by-side fighter-bomber was literally *forced* into the SAC scheme of manned-bomber capabilities. By 1965, the B-47s had been retired to the "boneyard," the B-52Cs and Fs were being retired rather than refurbished, and the B-58 was programmed to phase out by the end of the decade. The future of the manned bomber was largely in question. Defense Secretary Robert S. McNamara, with the cloud of Vietnam lingering heavily over military decisions, budgets, and emotions, stated in 1964: "Various options are open for replacing the B-52s in the 'seventies, if a replacement requirement exists at that time. In case supersonic speed and high altitude are needed for the future strategic bomber, the experience gained from three different Mach 3 planes, currently in the research and development stage, will be available—the XB-70, the A-11 and the SR-71." In actuality, the B-70 materialized only in the form of two prototypes, the A-11 was not pursued (it could not have been seriously considered as a strategic bomber in the first place), and the SR-71 (a derivative of the A-11) became a productive reconnaissance platform. McNamara went on to say, "In case low-level penetration capabilities turn out to be the key to future bomber effectiveness, the lessons being learned from the F-111, for example, will be applicable." (Perhaps of no small significance, the F-111 was being built in Texas, the home of President Lyndon B. Johnson.)

The next year (8 December 1965), Secretary McNamara announced that all B-58s and the B-52Cs, Ds, Es, and Fs would be phased out by June 1971. The announcement would mean the eventual disposal of 449 B-52 bombers, but continued employment of the "D" models in Vietnam delayed their retirement—and the remaining "Fs"—until 1978.

Reflect for a moment on Secretary McNamara's 8 December 1965 projection to "replace" the B-52 in the 1970s. Some "35-plus" years later, the venerable and durable B-52 is *still* flying and *still* a vital part of US war-planning and war-fighting strategy. Sixty-six of these bombers, equipped as ALCM carriers, are projected to be around until at least the year 2020!

On 10 December 1965, McNamara announced that the Department of Defense would budget for the purchase of 210 FB-111s. A spin-off of the controversial TFX or F-111, the FB-111 was to "replace" the retiring B-47 and B-58 fleets, and the older B-52s. The Navy had already rejected the F-111 for failing to meet the limitations and requirements of its carrier operations. Two months into the Nixon administration, on 19 March 1969, Secretary of Defense Melvin Laird announced that the FB-111 procurement would be limited to 60 operational aircraft and "a few" replacement aircraft. He said the FB-111 did not meet the requirements for an inter-continental bomber, but that the government was committed to purchase 60 of them to "salvage" the invested cost.

The first FB-111 was delivered to the 43d Bomb Group at Carswell AFB on 8 October 1969. Preceded by the B-36 and the B-58, the FB-111 became the third "new-type" bomber delivered to the SAC base from the General Dynamics plant next door. The new "medium" strategic bomber had two Pratt & Whitney TF-30-P-7 engines capable of delivering 20,350 lbs of thrust with afterburner. The aircraft was relatively small, with a fuselage length of approximately 73 feet, a fully extended wingspan of 70 feet, a fully swept wingspan of 33 feet, 11 inches, and a gross weight of 100,000 lbs. It was designed to fly at speeds up to Mach 2.5 at 36,000 feet. It had a service ceiling of 60,000 feet and a range of 4,100 miles (with external tanks). The bomber's delivery capability included up to four SRAM air-to-surface missiles on external pylons and two in the bomb bay; or six gravity nuclear bombs, or a combination of missiles and bombs.

The last FB-111 was delivered on 30 June 1971, after which the fighter-bombers were dispersed to two operational wings: the 509th Bombardment Wing at Pease AFB, New Hampshire, and the 380th Bombardment Wing at Plattsburgh AFB, New York. The 340th Bomb Group was subsequently inactivated.

Having nothing else to back up the rapidly depleting manned bomber leg of the Triad, SAC reluctantly accepted the FB-111 as a strategic bomber. General LeMay had fought the suggestion to buy the FB-111 from the time it was made. He argued that it was "not a long-range bomber" and, with only two engines, it lacked the payload-carrying capacity to deliver an adequate number of weapons for the incurred cost. The incurred cost being, amongst other things, "too many refueling tankers to support its combat missions." To partially mitigate the aircraft's range limitations, they were positioned on the northeast coast requiring a shorter mission and fewer tankers to reach Soviet targets.

According to Lt Gen (then Col) Dick Burpee, one of the early FB-111 wing commanders, the lives of the Cold Warriors who maintained and flew the FB-111s were difficult at best. First, the attitude of senior staff officers at Headquarters SAC generally reflected that of General LeMay: the aircraft simply wasn't a long-range strategic bomber, and it required far too much attention and detail to employ it in training and combat missions. All of the tactical directives employing SAC bombers were written for the B-52; they did not fit the FB-111.

Burpee went on to conclude that, while the "little" bomber could not carry the payload of the B-52, and while it was also a maintenance and reliability "nightmare," it had excellent bombing accuracy when it *did* get to a target area. Its navigation systems, carried over from its fighter heritage and designed to run for 20 hours between parts failures, were lucky to operate for four hours; and spare parts for the FB-111 received the lowest priority in the SAC maintenance scheme of things. In the early operating days of the little fighter-bomber, at least five "cannibalizations" (removing and using parts from other aircraft) were the norm in getting a sortie under way.

Reportedly, the FB-111's maintenance reliability was so bad that when one bomb wing was scheduled for an operational readiness inspection (ORI), the other wing provided spare parts. The parts were "rushed" to a rendezvous point at White River Junction, New Hampshire, (a midpoint between the two wings' operating locations) for the wing undergoing inspection to pick them up.

The major complaint was that SAC Headquarters was so indifferent to FB-111's role that the two operating units were virtually left to their own devices to remain combat ready. Yet, the two units were required to respond to the same rigorous taskings and evaluations that the "trusted" B-52, KC-135, and ICBM units had to respond to—and in the same professional manner!

There was also an assertion that undue pressure was placed on the FB-111 units. During one six-month period, for example, the 509th Bomb Wing was subjected to three readiness inspections—by the 8th Air Force Inspector General, the SAC Inspector General, and the Headquarters Air Force Inspector General. Overkill? Probably!

General Burpee relates a story about being called in to discuss FB-111 reliability problems with Gen John C. Meyer, then commander of SAC. After Burpee explained that the FB-111's reliability problem was purely a lack of spare parts and higher headquarters apathy about the bomber, the CINC commented that it was hard for him to distinguish between the unfortunate and the incompetent. This audience with the SAC leader left a young wing commander despondent at the time; but to his surprise, and in a matter of a few days, there was a sudden interest in the welfare and utility of the "ugly duckling" FB-111. The two FB-111 "lonely stepchildren" bomb wings suddenly found themselves in the limelight of attention and support. Thereafter, the FB-111, though still "suspect" as a real contributor to the strategic nuclear forces, received the necessary attention and support to maintain combat reliability. Burpee concludes the story:

> The Cold Warriors who flew and maintained the FB-111 never had their spirits broken or never failed to perform their duty. They maintained the nuclear alert status and learned how to bomb without any automatic navigation and radar aids. They could do this and still get "reliable bombs by B-52 standards." Before the FB-111 was finally retired from the SAC bomber force, it had received the most modern advanced bombing and navigation upgrades and became a highly reliable and skilled precision bomber. Though it never gained the respect of the heavy bomber "mafia," it did contribute greatly to Cold War deterrence.

The *B-1*. Soon after his inauguration, President Ronald Reagan directed "resurrection" of the controversial B-1 strategic bomber that had been canceled by President Carter. The Carter administration had opted to shift US deterrent strategy in favor of the more survivable standoff cruise missile. The Reagan decision was undoubtedly more internationally political than militarily practical. He wanted to send a strong message to the Soviets that his pre-election declarations were more than rhetoric.

Unfortunately, Rockwell International and dozens of supporting industry contractors had all but dismantled the tooling and the organization that had been designed to build the bomber. Four preproduction B-1 bombers had been built, however, and all original design requirements had been met. Operational test flights had demonstrated its ability to fly at Mach 2, fast-react for base escape, penetrate at high and low altitudes and at high speeds, fire and control both gravity and cruise missile weapons, and maintain a stable air refueling capability. The B-1's defensive avionics, frequency surveillance, and warning and electronic countermeasures were at the most modern state-of-the-art level. The bomber's four General Electric F101-GE-100 afterburner turbofan engines were capable of delivering 30,000 lbs of thrust. The crew consisted of two pilots and two offensive systems operators (navigator-bombardier and electronic warfare controller).

The bomber had a fuselage length of 150 feet, 2½ inches, a fully extended wingspan of 136 feet, 8½ inches, a fully swept-back wingspan of 78 feet, 2½ inches, and a gross weight of 389,800 lbs. The B-1 had a design speed of Mach 2.1 at 50,000 feet and an unrefueled range of 6,100 miles. Its weapon delivery capability included three internal bomb bays, which could accommodate either 24 SRAMs on rotary dispensers or 75,000 lbs of gravity bombs.

The revived B-1 program called for essentially the same configuration and performance requirements as the original versions, which were based on early 20-year-old design technology. The revised production program encountered two major problems:

1. The cost of the bomber rose exponentially with the retooling and reorganizing required after a four-year hiatus.

2. The aircraft presented multiple problems with fuel leaks, electronics, and overall performance. Although being flown by combat crews in two bomb wings, the B-1 was integrated into the SIOP for only a few years before being negotiated out as part of a nuclear arms reduction program.

The Tanker

A major contributor to the concept of flexible response and extra-long-range bomber planning was the development of aerial refueling. SAC moved rapidly from the "probe and drogue" flexible hose concept passed on from the Royal Air

Force (RAF) to the largest, most reliable, and most efficient air refueling force in the world. The venerable World War II B-29 became the first air refueling "tanker." It was followed by KB-50A and, finally, an aircraft fully developed as an aerial tanker—the KC-97. Described briefly below are the various configurations of the SAC tanker fleet subsequent to the modified B-29 and B-50.

KC-97 Stratotanker. SAC's first "designed" tanker, the KC-97 Stratotanker evolved from the Boeing *Stratocruiser* commercial airliner of the 1950s and, later, the Air Force transport version, the C-97. The Air Force began purchasing KC-97 tankers in 1950. By 1958, the inventory included 780 of these aircraft; they remained in service until 1965. The KC-97 had an operating range of 4,300 miles—an excellent range, considering that it had to burn 115/145 aviation gas in its engines while carrying JP-4 for off-loading to B-47s and B-52s. The tanker's main limitations were in altitude and airspeed: The bombers had to descend to low altitudes in order to rendezvous with the KC-97, and they had to fly slowly in order to "hook-up" with the tanker. These requirements caused the bombers to burn much more fuel than they burned at their usual higher altitudes and higher speeds.

The *KC-135*. Also derived from a Boeing-built commercial airliner (the 707), the KC-135 became SAC's first all-jet tanker. First test-flown as a tanker on 31 August 1956, it became operational less than a year later, on 28 June 1957; it is still flying actively today, 30 years later. The tanker is capable of off-loading 120,000 lbs of fuel and flying a range of 3,000 miles. The original 135s were equipped with the basic Pratt & Whitney J-47 engine with water injection to assist in takeoff. Later, the J-57 was installed; it stood the test for 25 years before being replaced in 1981 by the CFM-56 turbofan engine at a cost of approximately $4 million per aircraft ($1 million per engine).

The Air Force Reserve Forces, operating KC-135s in direct support of SAC and other Air Force components, upgraded their tankers with the less expensive (but much improved over the original) JT-3D-3B turbofan engine. Both engines were predicted to extend the KC-135's life to 27,000 flying hours and the year 2020. Boeing delivered a total of 820 KC-135 tankers, several of which were converted to RCs (for reconnaissance) or ECs (for airborne command and control and electronic warfare operations).

SAC brought women into KC-135 flight operations in the early 1980s, first as copilots, navigators, boom operators, and crew chiefs. The copilots eventually became aircraft commanders. The first "all-female" KC-135 crew flew an operational mission on 10 June 1982. Capt Kelly S. C. Hamilton, SAC's first female KC-135 aircraft commander, with copilot Lt Linda Martin and instructor navigator Capt Cathy Bacon, navigator Lt Diane Oswald, and boom operator Sgt Jackie Hale, off-loaded fuel to a B-52 in a five-hour training mission. SAC noted that the flight was "token" in nature and would not become the norm; developing a program of all-female crews would in fact defeat the whole concept of integrating women into all phases of combat crew operations.

My experience with the KC/EC-135, having logged over three thousand hours in the two configurations, was a pleasant one. I thoroughly enjoyed flying the airplane. It was a joy to make instrument approaches and landings in the 135—and as the improved engines came along, it became an even greater pleasure. The 135 has become the latter-day C-47 "Gooney Bird" of the Air Force, having flown actively and in large numbers for forty years—and it has a projected life of another 25 years or more!

KC-10 *Extender.* McDonnell Douglas won the competition to develop and produce an extended-range tanker for the Air Force. The KC-10 is a derivative of the commercial DC-10, a tri-jet passenger plane. Following modification of the basic aircraft, the KC-10 could carry a total of 367,847 lbs of jet fuel—117,829 in newly installed bladder tanks in the lower fuselage bay area, the remainder in wing tanks. The KC-10 was capable of off-loading 200,000 lbs of fuel up to 2,200 miles from its launch base and then returning home.

Other major changes to the basic DC-10 included installation of a telescoping air refueling boom and a boom operator position in the lower aft belly. The position could accommodate up to three crew members—boom operator, student, and instructor. The cockpit configuration remained essentially the same as the commercial version—pilot, copilot, and engineer or navigator. The aircraft was also modified to take on fuel from another tanker, thereby extending its range for refueling, cargo delivery, or passenger missions. The first of fifty KC-10s was delivered on 15 September 1982. No complaints were heard from the fortunate young tanker warriors who received assignments to the new airplane.

Reconnaissance

Keeping a vigilant eye on the enemy—by whatever means— is the oldest form of intelligence collection. Strategic reconnaissance becomes necessary when access to the enemy's borders (or to contacts within its territory) is denied, or when the validity of information obtained by agents or extracted from emigres is in doubt. Aerial reconnaissance by specially equipped aircraft or satellites is the essence of strategic reconnaissance. Long-range aerial reconnaissance dates back to the US Civil War, when crude balloons were used to spy on the enemy from above. Balloon reconnaissance came into its own in World War I, as did airplane reconnaissance. Ground activity below could be observed and information about that activity could be brought back to the field commander.

During World War II, the British and the Germans used aerial photography to document and report enemy movements. From their airborne platforms, they could also hear radio transmissions more clearly. These were the earliest forms of photo intelligence (PHOTINT), and communications intelligence (COMINT). The Cold War and the emerging technologies that accompanied it—dedicated reconnaissance aircraft and dedicated collection means—opened a new frontier. Signals intelligence (SIGINT), which includes telemetry intelligence (TELINT), and electronic intelligence (ELINT), entails the monitoring and collection of nonimaging electromagnetic radiation.

Telemetry guidance signals emanating from missiles and rockets are picked up by TELINT; radar emissions are the main signals picked up by ELINT. Technological advances and refinements in each of these disciplines have continued to escalate, which has generated a growing demand for better and more precise information. Major diplomatic, policy, strategic, and tactical decisions are based on collected and interpreted information derived from strategic reconnaissance. Strategic reconnaissance "grew up" with the Cold War. The United States with its allies, and the Soviet Union with its allies, matched wits throughout the Cold War period, evolving collection means and increasing defenses against detection. After the U-2 piloted by Gary Powers was shot down in 1960, both sides refined their activities. Both became even more sophisticated and both developed greater finesse; and to a large extent, both became less provocative.

SAC and the Navy began developing greater strategic reconnaissance capabilities immediately after World War II. Better strategic reconnaissance was needed to support their strategic charter, which increased their planning requirements. By 1948, SAC had two strategic reconnaissance groups of converted bombers, including 24 RB-17s and 30 RB-29s, for long-range aerial surveillance and information collection. Later, the RB-36 and the RB-47 joined the reconnaissance mission. Specially stripped "light-weight" RB-36s could range over areas of interest at altitudes of 55,000 feet, well above the MiG-15s' ceiling at the time. Each of the converted bombers utilized pressurized compartments in the bomb bay areas to accommodate specially trained SIGINT and PHOTINT operators and their equipment. In 1962, SAC took delivery of its first RC-135 reconnaissance platform. Thereafter, "several" KC-135s were converted to RCs in numerous configurations. The RC-135 provided space for equipment installations, external antennas, and working areas for operators and technicians. It also had the range necessary to accomplish its missions from operating bases around the world.

The RC-135 was a welcome relief for the crews that had flown for years in the cramped and cold RB-47 bomb bay "pod." The Navy began reconnaissance activities in Europe and the Far East, flying converted PB4Y Privateers (an outgrowth from the Air Force B-24), along with Lockheed P2V Neptunes and Martin P4M Mercators. Later, the Navy operated the Lockheed EC-121 and EP-3B *Orion* in a variety of ocean and overland surveillance, photo, and signals collection roles. The EA-3B twin-jet reconnaissance aircraft operated from both carriers and land-based runways, primarily for SIGINT operations. Suffice to say, all reconnaissance missions were highly classified, including the various types of onboard collection equipment and capabilities. Therefore, these unsung Cold Warriors did not receive the publicity or recognition accorded the other war-fighting forces. These "intelligence warriors" often encountered more of a "Hot War" than a Cold War in carrying out their assigned missions. They flew against armed and hostile *targeted* surveillance areas as well as under severe environmental flying conditions. The "Recce" forces frequently had to absorb their tragedies quietly, and to grieve privately over the losses of fellow crewmen, because the losses could not be publicly acknowledged due to mission classification and sensitivity.

SAC and Navy units consistently exercised the right to operate over international waters, much to the dismay and frustration of the Soviets, the Chinese, the North Koreans, and the Cubans. The "Recce" warriors continued to fly, even at the risk of hostile action—which *did* occur! Nor did the Soviets limit their hostile action to actual "Recce" aircraft; they shot down two Korean airliners, one over the Barents Sea (which crash-landed in Northern Russia), and Korean Air 007 (which crashed in the Sea of Japan with 269 passengers and crew aboard). The belief is that the airliners were falsely identified as US reconnaissance aircraft.

At least 70 SAC and Navy "Recce" aviators were lost during the period. However, due to the sensitivity and continued classification of US reconnaissance operations, I will limit this segment to a brief description of two other dedicated reconnaissance aircraft.

The *U-2*. The first worldwide awareness of the U-2 came when Gary Powers was shot down over the Soviet Union in 1960. Six years earlier, in 1954, the Central Intelligence Agency (CIA) had given the legendary "Kelly" Johnson of Lockheed Aircraft's "Skunk Works" the task of developing a high-altitude, extremely long-range reconnaissance aircraft. Richard Bissell, the agency's "spy plane guru," worked closely with Lockheed and Johnson in designing the new aircraft. It was dubbed "U" for "utility" to disguise any particular interest in the engineering development and manufacture of the airplane. By 1 August 1955, the first U-2 was ready to fly. It had a short fuselage and a wingspan of 80 feet, which made it difficult to keep the aircraft on the ground during the takeoff roll. Its bicycle-type landing gear was designed to retract into the fuselage. It had outrigger "pogo stick" wheels that were used for takeoff, then dropped when the plane became airborne. The U-2 was fully conceived under the auspices of the CIA and was "developed from scratch" to be a "spy plane." The initial program called for 30 airplanes at a cost of $35 million. The first U-2 pilots, recruited from the Air Force and the Navy, resigned their commissions and became Lockheed employees to protect their military backgrounds and their mission. Also, they had been "sheep dipped" by the CIA to expunge their military backgrounds. The initial intended use of the U-2 was to support the Eisenhower "Open Skies" initiative, which Khrushchev rejected.

Given the resources to conduct surveillance of Soviet ICBM developments, however, and with persistent assertions of a "missile gap," CIA Director Allen Dulles, supported by Secretary of Defense Thomas Gates, convinced the president that overflight missions ought to be conducted anyway. When he approved the first deep-Russia U-2 overflight, President Dwight Eisenhower gave a prophetic admonition to CIA Director Dulles and U-2 manager Bissell: "Well boys, I believe the country needs this information and I'm going to approve it. But I'll tell you one thing. Someday one of these machines is going to get caught and we're going to have a storm."

On 1 July 1956, the first U-2 intelligence-gathering flight flew over Moscow, Leningrad, and the Baltic Seacoast. The Soviets detected the U-2, but could not intercept it at its extreme high altitude. Its vast PHOTINT capability photographed a seven-mile-wide path and brought back phenomenal "real-time" photographic coverage of Russia. The Soviets at first lodged secret protests with the State Department. Later, they were more vocal with the US Embassy in Moscow, demanding that the United States stop the intrusions. Nikita Khrushchev continued to protest thereafter—until the Powers incident.

The first U-2s were delivered to SAC in June 1957, at the 4028th Strategic Reconnaissance Squadron, Laughlin AFB, in far Southwest Texas, where transition training took place. The

Air Force's initial experience with the U-2 was a near-disaster—five SAC pilots and two Lockheed pilots killed in the first year of operation. Eventually, however, the U-2's mechanical defects were worked out and the aircraft became a reliable collection platform. It continues to operate today, along with its advanced successor, the TR-1.

I was privileged to enjoy a couple of "dollar rides" in the U-2 while serving as commander of the 12th Air Division, to which the parent reconnaissance aircraft wing was assigned. The thrill of the "slingshot" takeoff and the climb to 80,000 feet was an exhilaration I had never before experienced—nor ever after—not to mention the several "porpoising" touch-and-go landings that followed. Flights such as this by senior commanders were mostly symbolic, demonstrating to the "troops" their interest in the systems. But they were also important from the point of view of "living" in the environment—if only briefly. Each event in the U-2 experience deepened my respect for the young fellows who "squeeze" and contort their pressure-suited bodies into the cramped cockpit and sit routinely for 12-plus hours, flying incredible missions.

SR-71 *Blackbird*. The success of the U-2 prompted the CIA to contract the same team to develop a collection platform that could cruise at even higher altitudes and at supersonic speeds. The initial A-12, created by "Kelly" Johnson's team, was completed in January 1962; it flew on 26 April. The huge delta wing twin-engine aircraft was generations ahead in design, material technologies, and engine propulsion. These factors combined to revolutionize aircraft speed and altitude. The CIA bought fifteen of the A-12s, single-seaters with sensor equipment operated by the pilot. The Air Force gave some early consideration to buying the A-12 (YF-12) for use as an interceptor, but opted instead for the SR-71, a "two-seat" reconnaissance platform.

The addition of the second cockpit and a reconnaissance systems officer (RSO) greatly relieved the pilot's workload and further amplified the aircraft's capabilities. The SR-71 program and its operations remain highly classified, with most of the aircraft now resting on display pedestals around the country.

The Intercontinental Ballistic Missile - ICBM

SM-65 Atlas. The Air Force and SAC won the battle for management, deployment, and command and control of the land-based strategic ICBM programs. The first missile assigned to SAC, the Snark ground-to-ground system, was followed by the Thor ground-to-ground system, was followed by the intermediate range ballistic missile (IRBM) with a 1,900-mile nuclear warhead delivery range. The Thor, developed and manufactured in the United States, was provided to the United Kingdom's Royal Air Force, and to Italy and Turkey, as part of NATO's nuclear deterrence strategy. SAC conducted Thor crew training for the NATO Allies at Vandenberg AFB. In 1961, SAC and NATO jointly operated 30 Thor missile squadrons across Europe.

The first Atlas squadron was activated on 1 February 1958 at Francis E. Warren AFB, Wyoming. Atlas was the first truly intercontinental ballistic missile, having a range of five thousand miles. It was also very large and cumbersome, measuring 75 feet in height and 10 feet in diameter. With a single warhead, it had a liftoff weight in excess of 300,000 lbs. President Eisenhower, in response to the pressures of the "missile gap" hysteria, put a high priority on developing and deploying the Atlas; it became the personal project of Maj Gen Bernard Schriever. The system moved rapidly from research and development to operational in just three years—a phenomenal feat, considering the technologies required to field such a mammoth system. By 1962, SAC had 142 Atlas ICBMs deployed; with Titan I and II and Minuteman developments proving successful, however, all the Atlas weapons system missiles were retired by June 1965. The *Atlas* remained for years thereafter as an important heavy-payload launch vehicle.

LGM-25 *Titan I* and *Titan II.* The two-stage heavy ICBM development program, begun in 1955, followed the success of Atlas. Martin Company won the contract to build the Titan system and launched the first missile on 6 February 1959. The first four test launches were successful, but the next two test missiles exploded on the launch pad. Thereafter, the program was deemed successful and development proceeded. The Titan, which measured 110 feet in length with the warhead attached, was 10 feet in diameter at the first stage and 8 feet in diameter at the second stage. The missile's Aerojet XLR91-AJ liquid propellant engine burned a mixture of hydrazine and nitrogen tetroxide. With a one-minute countdown sequence from launch initiation, it lifted a weight of 300,000 lbs with a total thrust of 530,000 lbs, sending it (inertially guided) toward its target at 17,000 MPH to a range in excess of six thousand miles. Its four-megaton warhead, the largest in SAC's nuclear arsenal, had a target strike accuracy of less than a mile. The SAC inventory reached a peak of 63 Titan Is and 56 Titan IIs deployed in 1963. The Titan I was fully deactivated in 1965 as the Minuteman systems came on line, and the last Titan II complex was deactivated in 1985. Thus was the era of liquid-propelled, heavy ICBMs in the US war plan brought to an end.

LGM-30A, B, & F *Minuteman I, II,* and *III.* Boeing's Minuteman ICBM was designed specifically as a strategic weapon system, unlike Atlas and Titan, which were basically space launch vehicles first and weapon systems second. The system's engine burns solid propellant, thereby negating the requirement for collocated launch/maintenance crews. The ideal configuration design—continuous system remote check-out, missiles placed in vertical launchers, and combat crews monitoring ten missiles concurrently—took SAC into "push-button warfare," with near instantaneous response. The dispersal of the missile silos and launch control centers along highways (and off-highway roads) contributes to security and ease of maintenance. The basic Minuteman design is simpler, lower in cost, and safer than the earlier liquid-propelled engine systems—and it will not become obsolete in the near future.

The concept of Minuteman is similar to the early arsenal practice of having cartridges and ammunition that will not deteriorate rapidly and can therefore be stockpiled and kept ready for use. SAC eventually deployed one thousand Minuteman missiles within six wing complexes in the western and midwestern United States. The basic missile, which measures 54 to 60 feet in length and 6 feet in diameter, operates with a continuously running inertial guidance system. Reaction time from launch initiation is less than 60 seconds, including automatic opening of the launcher sliding door. With a 120,000-lb thrust, the missile can project its warhead 5,500 miles to the target. ICBM systems brought a new and different dimension to SAC's combat crew force.

The Cruise Missile

To provide a multiple mission capability to its war-planning strategies, the Air Force developed and deployed several types of air-to-ground attack missiles with the bomber force. The GAM-77/AGM-28 Hound Dog was designed as a standoff weapon to "soften" defenses or target complexes up to seven hundred miles away as the bomber penetrated enemy territory. The Hound Dog, operational with the B-52G and H models from 1961 to 1976, was equipped with an internal navigation guidance system that was updated to its actual position and its intended course of flight just prior to launch from the B-52. The missile could be programmed to fly to its target at speeds up to Mach 2.1 and at altitudes from treetop level to 55,000 feet. It was also unique in that its J-52 engine could be used to augment the bomber's power in flight and its fuel tanks could be topped off from the B-52's fuel system prior to launch. The GAM-87 Skybolt air-launched ballistic missile, developed by Douglas Aircraft Company, Aerojet General, General Electric, and Nortronics, came into the inventory in 1959 following a controversial decision process. Programmed to be carried by the B-52 and the British Vulcan bomber, the missile consisted of a two-stage solid propellent engine that could fly at hypersonic speeds to targets up to 1,000 miles from the launch point. Similar to the Hound Dog strategy, it was designed to be a "roll-back" weapon by the penetrating bomber force. The Skybolt, never a favorite of Secretary McNamara due to its checkered development tests and cost overruns, was canceled just as it was proving to be a reliable weapon.

As Soviet air defenses proliferated, making bomber penetration more of a concern, the Air Force turned to another air-to-ground missile to support the B-52s and FB-111s. The

AGM-69A SRAM, developed by General Dynamics, was selected to follow the defeated Skybolt in the early 1970s. The SRAM was also developed as a semiballistic air-launched missile with a Minuteman III equivalent warhead capability. The B-52 could carry up to 20 SRAMs mounted externally and internally, and could launch the missiles up to one hundred miles to a target. Its exceptionally short flight time of nominally "three minutes" (due to its hypersonic rocket engine) made it virtually invulnerable to radar tracking and interception by air defenses. SAC ultimately integrated 1,500 SRAMs into the SIOP bomber mission.

Shortly after his inauguration in the Spring of 1977, President Carter canceled production of the B-1 bomber in favor of developing a long-range cruise missile. The ALCM was given the highest priority for weapon system program development, in turn drastically modifying the Triad's strategic bomber leg mission. The ALCM meant that no new strategic bombers would be built and that the B-52 would become the cruise missile delivery vehicle, as it had been for the Hound Dog and SRAM air-to-ground missiles. The major difference was that the ALCM would be a "long-range" missile capable of low-level flight to its target after being launched outside enemy air defenses. A competitive flyoff between an airborne version of the already operational General Dynamics AGM-109 Tomahawk sea-launched cruise missile (SLCM) and a long-range version of Boeing's AGM-86A resulted in a win for the AGM-86. Boeing won the competitive selection process and was awarded a contract to develop the AGM-86B ALCM, a small unmanned vehicle powered by the 600-lb static thrust Williams F107-WR-100 turbofan engine and fitted with retractable wings. The ALCM's guidance system relied upon both inertial and preprogrammed navigation systems. The preprogrammed terrain matching and comparison system (TERCOM) can fly the missile and deliver a nuclear warhead up to 500 MPH and at extremely low altitudes, avoiding traditional radar detection en route to its target 1,500 miles into enemy territory.

The B-52G was the first bomber to be equipped with the ALCM (12 missiles, fitted externally under the wings). This configuration allowed the bomber to launch its missiles safely outside enemy radar detection and then to penetrate at low level and deliver its internally carried gravity bombs. The B-52G (and later, the B-52H) was modified to carry a rotary launcher within the bomb bay with an additional eight ALCMs in place of gravity weapons. This latter strategy allowed the bomber to carry 20 ALCM nuclear weapons, each launched before enemy territory had been penetrated, thereby substantially reducing the risk to aircraft and crew. While Carter's decision to rely more heavily on the cruise strategy than on the manned penetrating bomber was contentious among bomber advocates, the ALCM later proved to virtually overwhelm Soviet defense strategies. The small missiles (20 feet, 9 inches in length, two feet in diameter, with an extended wingspan of 12 feet), when launched in massive numbers, were capable of saturating Soviet target areas, virtually negating any reasonably cost-effective defense measures.

Close behind the ALCM came the development of the ground-launched cruise missile (GLCM). Utilizing the ALCM's basic design features, navigation systems, and engine, the GLCM could be launched from a transporter erector launcher (TEL) and fly 1,500 miles to a target. SAC was given the GLCM mission, and was authorized to purchase 464 GLCMs for deployment with NATO's theater nuclear forces in Europe. The Soviet defense structure was complicated still further and the balance of power was greatly swayed—a factor that would provide an important SALT "bargaining chip" in the 1980s.

The Fleet Ballistic Missile Submarine - SSBN

The Navy had begun work on nuclear-driven submarine technology as early as 1947, under the leadership of Capt Hyman G. Rickover. Four years into the design phase of a nuclear submarine, the Electric Boat Company of General Dynamics was placed under contract to build the first reactor-powered submarine. The Mark II thermal reactor power system was chosen as the "engine." The keel for the first boat, the *Nautilus,* was laid in June 1952; the submarine was launched on 21 January 1954.

The first sea voyage test of the new submarine commenced on 17 January 1955 under the command of Capt Eugene P. Wilkinson with a pensive Rear Admiral Rickover anxiously watching the proceedings. The nuclear-powered submarine performed perfectly, quickly proving that the new power source could drive submarines of virtually any size to unlimited distances. In the first 2½ years, the *Nautilus* traveled 62,000 miles—unrefueled and on its first uranium reactor core! In July 1958, four years after *Nautilus* was commissioned, Capt William R. Anderson guided her from Seattle, Washington, to Portland, England, traveling under the Arctic ice pack.

Nautilus was only a prototype—but with the proof-of-concept for a nuclear-powered submarine "solved," the Navy set about investigating the possibility that IRBMs and ICBMs could be launched from a submarine. But the Navy's attempts to solicit cooperative support from the Air Force and the Army failed. The Air Force had no inclination to join the Navy in developing a system that would require new techniques designed to accommodate underwater launches. The Army initially joined in a project with the Navy to develop the Jupiter IRBM, but the liquid-propelled engine was not really compatible with submarine operations.

The Navy therefore began to develop its own missile, the Polaris. With DOD approval, the FBM program to develop the Polaris got under way in 1956. The program costs would be astronomical—$120 million for each submarine, with an estimated $10 billion to build and maintain the estimated 41-submarine fleet. (This is without the cost of the yet-to-be developed Polaris SLBM.) The goal for the submarine-launched missile was for a solid propellant, two-stage, vertically chambered ballistic missile that could launch from safe ocean areas and strike most strategic targets within the Soviet Union. The missile's warhead would have to be both lightweight and powerful.

Concurrent with the development of the nuclear-powered submarine and the appropriately sized SLBM, the Atomic Energy Commission (AEC) was working on smaller weapons for use by Air Force fighter-bombers and Army missiles. The defense electronics industry was also perfecting miniature inertial navigation units for ballistic missiles, and Dr. Charles

Draper at Massachusetts Institute of Technology (MIT) was developing a precise navigation plotting system for submarine use. The Ship's Inertial Navigation System (SINS), when finally installed in the Nautilus, could accurately pinpoint the geographic location of the submerged submarine at any place under the ocean—a factor that was critical to a missile's onboard inertial guidance system for launching missiles. While Rickover was closely managing the SSBN development, Rear Adm William Raborn became the Navy's chief SLBM developer; he skillfully guided the creation of the entire Polaris system, component by component, until it became a reality.

The Navy "launched" into full production of SSBN boats—with continuing emphasis on deeper operational submarines, quieter engines, and larger SLBM capacities. The USS Lafayette was the first of 31 boats built to carry the Polaris A3 as well as the Poseidon C3 with MIRV warheads. The next class of SSBNs began with the USS Ohio's improved noise reduction characteristics and a capacity for carrying 24 SLBMs, including the Trident C4 and D5 missiles. It is important to mention that the Navy's nuclear attack submarines (SSN) also played important roles in the Cold War, not only as "hunters-trackers" of Soviet submarines and surface vessels, and as escorts for the boomer force, but also as offensive nuclear warriors. The SSN fleet is armed with a variety of tactical nuclear weapons, including the torpedo tube-launched Tomahawk and the Harpoon SLCM, with standoff ranges up to 1,400 miles and capabilities to strike targets well inside the Soviet Union.

Lafayette Class. Thirty-one boats were built during the 1960s and 1970s. The first eight were equipped with 16 Polaris A2 SLBMs; the remaining 23 could carry 16 Polaris A3 MIRV SLBMs. All were later converted to carry the Poseidon C4 missiles. The huge submarines, which measure 425 feet in length and 33 feet across the beam, have a submerged displacement of 8,250 tons. The boats have four 21-inch torpedo tubes for defensive operations. The 15,000-horsepower nuclear propulsion engine provides power through a single propeller shaft to achieve speeds of 20 knots on the surface and 30 knots submerged. The normal crew complement of the *Lafayette* class boats is 140. The last 12 boats were enlarged in size and given improved underwater "stealth" features. Referred to as *Benjamin Franklin*-class boats, the crew size was increased to 168. They can deliver the Trident C4 SLBM.

Ohio Class. The Navy launched the USS *Ohio* in 1979. Much larger than its predecessor, it measures 560 feet in length and 42 feet across the beam; it displaces 18,700 tons submerged. Like the *Lafayette*, the *Ohio*'s 60,000-horsepower nuclear engine delivers power through a single propeller shaft. The *Ohio*'s submerged speed is in excess of 30 knots and it carries a crew of 133. It also carries 24 Trident I C4 or Trident II D5 SLBMs.

UGM-27 Polaris A3. Sea-launched ballistic missiles have kept pace with nuclear submarine technology since the first Polaris A1 was developed in the late 1950s. The two-stage missile is 31 ft, 6 inches long, has a 54-inch diameter, weighs 35,000 lbs, and has a range of 2,855 miles. The Polaris A3, last in the series, has been retired and is no longer operational—with either the US Navy or the British Royal Navy.

UGM-73 *Poseidon C3*. All *Lafayette* and *Franklin* boats were originally outfitted with the Poseidon C3, a 65,000-pound, 34-foot by 74-inch, two-stage missile capable of reaching targets up to 3,230 miles away with a payload of ten 50Kt RVs or 2,485 miles away with 14 MIRV weapons. Operational since 1971, the *C3* has the same relative range as the Polaris, but with twice the payload and a 100% improvement in accuracy. The Poseidon gave way to the Trident weapon system in the late 1980s.

UGM-93 *Trident I C4/Trident II D5*. With the same dimensions as the Poseidon, the Trident I C4 weighs 70,000 lbs. It is a three-stage solid propellant missile capable of delivering eight Mark 4 100Kt MIRV weapons to targets up to 4,400 miles from its launch point. The *Lafayette* and *Franklin* boats were capable of carrying 16 Tridents, and the remaining *Ohio*-class boats currently carry 24 missiles. The British have built several new SSBNs to carry the Trident with their own warhead design.

SAC Alert Force Operations

The Soviets, who had not pursued strategic airpower under Stalin, began to demonstrate significant progress in the development of strategic bombers and ICBMs, and in space vehicles, as was dramatically demonstrated by sputnik in 1957. The immediate perception was that SAC airfields could be vulnerable to relatively short-warning-time attacks from incoming missiles. The United States, which had *driven* Cold War strategic policy for a decade, found itself in the position of responding to Soviet policy. SAC planners countered with the ground alert program. SAC grew steadily, to a peak of 3,207 tactical aircraft and 262,609 personnel by 1959. The command's personnel strength rose to 282,723 in 1962 as the Minuteman ICBM system came on line with its combat crew force.

This author recalled Gen George Washington's order during the crucial days of the Revolutionary War, "*Put none but Americans on guard tonight,*" as his B-36 crew was among the first to be placed on SAC ground alert on that first day of October in 1957. We were then introduced to the newly refurbished World War II base operations building at Biggs AFB, near El Paso, Texas. Most of SAC's combat-ready crews had pulled brief ground alert duty tours during rotation periods to Alaska, Guam, Spain, North Africa, and the United Kingdom. But they had not pulled ground alert duty at their home base, except for the two- or three-day stint during the Hungary crisis in 1956. And those earlier experiences were for predetermined periods. They were also "novel"; that is, welcome changes in our routine. This "new" duty became a challenging experience for combat crew, support teams, and their families. The frequency of ground alert schedules initially was not terribly rigorous. We sort of "slipped" into the routine, slowly and without too much concern that this situation would continue for very long. Little did we suspect that the early alert confinement periods (24–72 hours) soon would become a steady routine of three full days (seven days eventually, and with ever-increasing frequency) of living within a tightly secured facility, often within a few miles of our homes and families. The ground alert posture was at first a new experience and, as such, it helped in fighting the boredom that soon set in.

As someone once said, "SAC alert tours amount to hours and days of boredom, punctuated by moments of stark terror and fear." The stark terror and fear occurred when the "klaxon horn" sounded; we had to get to our airplanes as rapidly as possible, get into our positions, turn on aircraft power, and prepare to start engines, to taxi, or to take off for war. The klaxon horn held a special agitation for alert crews: first, it was the most noxious and brain-freezing protracted spurt of noise ever devised and, second, its daunting signal could have meant any number of things—*all bad*. Fortunately, the million or more klaxon signals heard by Cold Warriors performing alert duty over the years ended in exercises that did not take the country to war.

Alert duty also often tested human interpersonal relationships to extreme limits. Getting along with a dozen or more people on a flight mission where everyone was personally engaged in his specialty was a far cry from living in close confinement with the same group day after day. Amazingly, though, in my own experience there was very little agitation between crew members; and when problems did occur, they were easily resolved. I served on the bomber crew force for ten years and the missile crew force for three years—and with only three different combat crews. The only crew member changes that occurred were those where an individual was given an opportunity to upgrade to a position of greater responsibility.

I often marveled then, and I reflect even more so today, at how well young officers (and some older ones) and enlisted men and women responded to those challenges—how truly professional they were! And, importantly, legions more of the same quality continued to follow the initial Cold Warriors—not drafted and not conscripted to train and serve in those tough and demanding jobs, they were all volunteers sincerely serving their country. This incredible process continued, literally for *generations* as sons came along to fly the same B-52 bomber or KC-135 tanker that their fathers had flown before them. As the ground alert posture persisted over the years, creature comforts continued to improve. The small black-and-white TVs were eventually replaced with current video technologies and movie releases; mess hall food became *gourmet* meals; all academic proficiency training was conducted while performing alert (as opposed to an extra duty after alert tours); and self-improvement correspondence courses were augmented with college-level classroom courses. The Minuteman Missile Education Program provided full-time graduate degree programs conducted by leading university faculties brought to the base. Of course, the enduring game of cards transcended all the years—bridge, poker, hearts, and many ingenious creations never before heard of, or thereafter!

The underpinning of the long days and *years* of standing alert was the seriousness of the requirement. There was the occasional "why don't they do it this way?" or "that way," but seldom "why are we doing this?" I regret only that there was not a greater attempt to characterize the "*why.*" Not that we did not accept the requirement to be there, but in my mind few really understood the deep ideological, cultural, and social differences in the world that brought the United States and the Soviet Union to that place. The issues were seldom discussed. The Soviet Cold Warriors, I have learned later, were broadly indoctrinated—perhaps not entirely forthrightly or truthfully, but they were given considerable words of motivating impetus to serve their cause. Larger factors than their lifestyles and social conditions, although never really tested, generally overcame personal motives at most levels to perform at very high standards. Hence, my motivation in this "Reflections" effort has been to review and recognize the many who served as Cold Warriors, and to inform those who were not so fortunate as to serve, that a great job was accomplished—and why!

In 1958, President Eisenhower directed that SAC begin dispersing its bombers to other Air Force (non-SAC) bases within the continental United States (CONUS). This maneuver was designed to further enhance US flexible response strategy—greatly in response to the *bomber gap* and *missile gap* perceptions—and to further complicate the Soviets' ICBM targeting problem.

Also in 1958, SAC adopted its paradoxical slogan, *Peace is Our Profession.* It was termed *paradoxical* by some who found it inconceivable that the proprietor of the world's largest nuclear weapon arsenal could characterize itself as a professional peacemaker! During the Christmas season of 1957, a 50-foot Christmas tree was erected in front of Headquarters SAC in Omaha. The bulbs were to be lighted one at a time, each reflecting a SAC airman who had agreed to reenlist before the end of the year. Civil engineering was called upon to place a sign on the tree, *Maintaining Peace is Our Profession;* but the sign painter found that he did not have enough space to accommodate all the words.

According to John Bohn, the venerable SAC historian, who unfortunately passed away in 1995, the project officers for the "Tree of Peace" project decided to drop the word "Maintaining" in the interest of space. Col Charley Van Vliet of Eighth Air Force liked the modified sign so much that he had a similar one erected over the main entrance to Westover AFB. As the *Peace is Our Profession* slogan began to show up at other SAC bases, the news media began to publish it as the SAC slogan and the command officially adopted it.

In the early 1960s, the airborne alert concept (Chromedome) was to be implemented after two years of testing. Gen Thomas S. Power, commander in chief, Strategic Air Command (CINCSAC) had testified before Congress in February 1959:

> We, in Strategic Air Command have developed a system known as airborne alert where we maintain airplanes in the air 24 hours a day, loaded with bombs, on station, ready to go to the target . . . I feel strongly that we must get on with this airborne alert . . . We must impress Mr. Khrushchev that we have it, and that he cannot strike this country with impunity.

Used effectively to stem the Cuban Crisis, the Chromedome tactic challenged the B-52 combat crew force to reach new heights: Take off fully loaded with fuel and nuclear weapons (a gross weight of almost 300,000 lbs), fly a predesignated route and refuel twice in the air (taking on 120,000 lbs of fuel during each refueling), and remain airborne until relieved approximately 25 hours later by the next Chromedome aircraft.

The key element of the Chromedome mission was to position the bombers in such standoff orbiting patterns that they could respond in a relatively short time to predesignated targets in the Soviet Union if directed by the NCA. These creative initiatives gave *new* meaning to flexible response: the ability to employ strategic weapons in a selective and controlled manner, as well as in full retaliation if warranted, while providing added survivability to the bomber and crew force. No strategy, however, can ignore the realities of force structure and performance—and they remained the key ingredients, provided by the steady influx of professional performers who came into the strategic forces to serve.

Several other initiatives, designed to enhance survivability and response, were taken during those apprehensive years. As SAC achieved a full one-third alert posture in May 1960 and followed with the continuous airborne command post operation Looking Glass in February 1961, a "full-up" command and control center was created onboard a converted KC-135 (Boeing 707) aircraft. These aircraft, designated "EC-135," were equipped with the latest and most advanced communications equipment. The flying command post remained in the air continuously, 24 hours per day. This amounted to three aircraft per day flying approximately eight or nine hour "shifts." The airborne aircraft could not land until properly relieved by a successor aircraft that was in the air and operationally ready to assume the command and control responsibilities—that is, to take control of the unbroken "communications link." Should the relief aircraft fail to take off due to maintenance, weather, or other problems, the airborne Looking Glass would be air-refueled by a standby alert tanker and continue on for another full airborne shift.

The Looking Glass could communicate with SAC forces worldwide as well as with the JCS command center, SAC underground command post, all unit command posts, and all SAC aircraft. By April 1967, Looking Glass crews possessed the capability to launch selected Minuteman ICBMs via an airborne launch control system (ALCS). A SAC general officer, with special training in emergency war order (EWO) implementation and in nuclear command and control procedures, was in command of each Looking Glass aircraft. This "airborne emergency actions officer" (AEAO), had authority to act for and on behalf of the commander in chief, SAC, in any confirmed wartime emergency. Indeed, should the president and the NCA become incapacitated, the AEOA could act for them.

The AEAO responsibilities constituted "additional duty" for these general officers—each had other day-to-day assignments, either within the SAC headquarters staff or as a numbered Air Force or Air Division commander stationed at a SAC base somewhere in the CONUS. These "field" generals would fly into

SAC headquarters and perform their AEAO duties for three or four days, then return to their primary jobs. If the general officer was also a pilot, he was required to become qualified in the EC-135 Looking Glass aircraft and to log a specified number of takeoffs, approaches, and landings in order to maintain proficiency. This added requirement delighted these particular AEAOs, since most of them had moved on beyond actively flying after being promoted to general officer.

Early in the Looking Glass program, the SAC generals assigned to AEAO duty were veterans of World War II and/or Korea. By the mid-1970s, virtually all SAC generals assigned to fly the airborne command post were Cold War veterans— former combat crew members from either the bomber, tanker, reconnaissance, or missile force. The post-attack command control system (PACCS), comprised of EC-135 aircraft, was closely coupled with Looking Glass. PACCS stood alert at designated SAC bases to augment the "Glass" during national emergencies. The PACCS aircraft would fly to preplanned orbit positions across the United States to form a "daisy chain" communications relay network. On 1 November 1975, SAC was given the added responsibility of managing the president's National Emergency Airborne Command Posts (NEAC). NEAC's aircraft included four E-4Bs (Boeing 747) equipped with communications systems common to Looking Glass and having the capability to span the frequency spectrum from very low frequency (VLF) to super high frequency (SHF). This capability allowed the onboard control team to have contact with virtually every nuclear weapons delivery system. The communications systems were also "hardened" against electro-magnetic pulse (EMP) effects.

The E-4B's automated data processing equipment provided the capability to process, store, display, and print command and control information. The data processing system was integrated with all strategic ground command, control, communications, and intelligence (C^4I) systems, greatly enhancing the onboard ability to direct strategic forces worldwide. The aircraft's large interior contains 4,350 square feet, divided into six separate working compartments. A large crew of specialists could operate and maintain the equipment array in support of the president and his staff when they were airborne during national emergencies.

The media promptly dubbed the E-4B the "Doomsday Plane." To exercise the NEAC systems, the E-4Bs were periodically integrated into the daily Looking Glass flying schedule, flying with the scheduled Glass crew aboard for that sortie. This was a pleasant departure from the normal EC-135 Looking Glass routine, and it provided a completely different onboard operating environment for the AEAO and the command and control team. The E-4B was truly a dream for SAC's Looking Glass teams to fly aboard and to operate. The huge aircraft's incredibly smooth stability in flight, and its spacious living conditions, were a far cry from the EC-135.

No one at the time of its implementation would have believed that the Looking Glass airborne alert operation would continue for almost 30 years—which it did! The operation was ongoing until 24 July 1990, when the United States became relatively confident that the threat of Soviet attack was no longer imminent.

The continuous airborne presence of the Looking Glass with a general officer and a war-fighting command and control team on board added immeasurably to the deterrence posture of the United States by giving the Soviet high command a constant worry regarding its potential intent. The Looking Glass mission has assumed a ground alert posture since 1990, with periodic airborne alert sorties to exercise the various systems and remain constantly ready.

Among other Cold War readiness initiatives implemented in 1961, the ground alert posture was increased to 50 percent of the bombers and tankers being combat-loaded and committed to a 15-minute takeoff response time. SAC combat crew members found even more demands on their lives with the escalating alert postures. The norm became seven days on alert, either in their home base alert facility or at a deployed base. When they came off alert, the crews would fly a 14- to 20-hour combat training mission that had been planned during the week on alert. Then they would get a few days of "free" time before repeating the routine—as soon as the next week in many cases. Looking back, I marvel at how it was all accomplished—by thousands of young men and women.

Morale was more than reasonably high, and retention rates of quality troops, both officers and enlisted personnel, remained the highest ever.

ICBM combat crew alert was yet another dimension of Cold Warrior dedication and performance. Though the concept of missiles was entirely new to SAC veterans, they adapted quickly to the ICBM weapon systems. Snark, Bomarc, Thor, Atlas, Titan, and Minuteman came into SAC operations as smoothly as new aircraft systems had come in over the years. New squadron and wing organizations were formed around the new weapon systems. Most of the new missile units took the designators of heroic World War II bomber wings, thus sustaining their heritage. SAC organized the missile combat crews in the same manner that had worked for years in the bomber and tanker crew force. Standardized, uniformed, and "numbered" combat crews were formed to meet the specific operational requirements of particular weapon systems—missile combat crew commander (MCCM), deputy crew commander, pilot, copilot, and so forth. And, just as in the air crew force, missile crews trained together, worked together, and lived together while honing their coordination in the same manner as a bomber crew with nuclear weapons in the bomb bay.

The number of crew members required to man an Atlas or Titan complex was four. The Minuteman combat crew consisted of two members. Atlas and Titan crews "lived" with their missiles, five Atlas to a complex and three Titan missiles to a complex. The liquid oxidizer and hyperbolic fuels of these ICBM systems required constant monitoring, care, and feeding. The later solid-propellant ICBMs—Minuteman and MX (Peacekeeper)—presented very few hazards to crew and maintenance operations. They were deployed in "clusters" or flights of 10 missiles, each connected electronically to a centrally located deep-underground launch control center (LCC). Rapid advances in ICBM technology led to the solid propellant "wooden concept" Minuteman missile, which required little day-to-day maintenance or upkeep. Only electronic monitoring of its constantly running guidance and control system and its launch-related electronic systems was required. Each two-man combat crew managed and controlled a flight of ten missiles that were deployed three-to-ten miles away and interconnected electronically with the LCC.

The rapid deployment of 1,000 Minuteman missiles over the period of a few short years in the early 1960s, while SAC was maintaining over a hundred Atlas missiles and 50-plus Titans on constant alert, required an incredible buildup of combat crew, maintenance, collateral support, and infrastructure personnel. The first Minuteman missile complex, two flights of ten missiles each, was declared combat-ready in November 1962; by 1966, SAC had 1,000 Minuteman missiles on alert. To aid in recruiting young officers from other specialties, SAC initiated the "Minuteman Missile Education Program" (MMEP). The program began at Malmstrom AFB, Montana, in 1962, coincident with the first Minuteman missiles coming up to alert status.

Regional and national universities participated, placing faculty at the six Minuteman missile wing locations in Montana, North Dakota, South Dakota, Wyoming, and Missouri. The universities offered post-graduate degrees in a variety of MBA and industrial management programs for combat crew members, all of whom were required to have a basic degree. The education program was an overwhelming success; it attracted top-notch young officers to the missile crew force, and it helped to offset boredom during the long hours of "sitting on alert." Individual course study and student dialogue took up the time slack in the "capsules."

I was in the process of rotating back to CONUS after four years of flying B-52Gs and performing ground and airborne alert in Puerto Rico when the MMEP attracted me. The selection system having "quickly" found me qualified and available, I was sent to Minuteman combat crew training and subsequently assigned to Ellsworth AFB, South Dakota, as a combat crew commander. Moving from the cockpit of a B-52 to a Minuteman LCC was an interesting cultural and "operating environment" change. However, other than operating a weapon system that didn't "taxi, take off, or fly," SAC procedures for managing, controlling, and employing nuclear weapons were identical to those in place for the B-52 mission—only the delivery vehicle was different.

Following ten years in the bomber crew force, I spent three years as a SAC combat crew Cold Warrior with the Minuteman. The missile crew adventure did not require a mad dash to a B-52; it required driving an Air Force automobile one hundred or more miles, often in snowstorms, to the LCC and the place of alert duty. Once on site, my "crew deputy" (Lt Bill Cisney) and I had to be identified by the security team and approved by the on-duty alert crew. We would then proceed to the elevator—and to the LCC, 60 feet below. When we arrived at the entrance to the console area, the on-duty crew would open the five-ton "blast door" and grant our entry into the 50-by-30-foot "cocoon." The changeover procedures between departing and oncoming crews was, in effect, a "change of command" with a status briefing on the missile flight, verification of the emergency war order documents, and symbolic exchange of responsibility between the old crew and the new crew. Any general rumors of upcoming events were passed on, of course, as were best wishes for a safe driving trip back home. We would then close the blast door, thereby "hardening" the capsule against nuclear damage in the event of an attack, complete the required operational preflight and communications checks, and prepare for the next 24 to 36 hours, when our relief crew would arrive to repeat the same process.

The ICBM alert duty tours always seemed to go quite smoothly. The main interruptions were occasional security alarms at the missile silos—usually when sensitive monitors had been set off by heavily blowing snow, a tumbleweed, or a rabbit. We would usually receive a message from either SAC or the Looking Glass airborne command post sometime during the duty period. Most often, the message would direct a practice launch exercise. And, sooner or later, the "dreaded" IG and his team of evaluators would descend upon us and conduct comprehensive readiness evaluations, thereby generating the "moments of stark terror" alluded to earlier.

ICBM alerts were every bit as tedious and demanding of the individual's competence, patience, professionalism, and dedication as were the bomber and tanker force requirements. Due to the long hours of isolation, and the potential for boredom, the Air Force Human Reliability Program applied a special emphasis on selecting, screening, and monitoring missile combat crew members. The program amounted to a very serious and comprehensive process of monitoring stress, unusual tendencies, behavioral "quirks," and potential marital discord. After almost 35 years of missile alert duty by thousands of bright Air Force officers, few were released from the assignment. These Cold Warriors served their country very well indeed. And the reliable ICBM weapons have never fired a shot in anger.

During my reading for this project, I happened across a *Newsweek* article entitled "Life With The Minuteman." Otherwise informative and accurate, the article contained this passage: "Although the warheads [of the Minuteman missile] can be disarmed by a radio command shortly after launch, nothing can stop the missile's flight." I wish to unequivocally correct that portion of the article. After a combat crew has received a valid launch message, all mandatory crosschecks, verifications, and safeguards are reviewed and authenticated, and the missile is launched toward its programmed target, **it cannot be disarmed!** (The only ICBMs that can be destroyed by the ground controller are those launched for test and exercise purposes and **are not** equipped with nuclear warheads.) If operational strategic systems could be electronically disarmed after a validated execution order, imagine what mischief the world's "wackos" could create—not to mention the "bogus" electronic signals interjected by enemy forces to disable the system.

For 34 consecutive years, from 1 October 1957 until 28 September 1991, SAC's combat crews stood alert, prepared to respond to their country's call to go to war, ready to defeat the ideological and military forces of the Soviet Union. In a 9 November 1957 memorandum to "Each member of the SAC Alert Force," General Power, CINCSAC, apprised SAC crews of the reasons for the ground alert posture and their purpose for being there:

> As a member of SAC's alert force, you are contributing to an operation which is of the utmost importance to the security of this nation and its allies in the free world. The purpose of this memorandum is to discuss with you some aspects of this operation and the importance of your part in it. For you must understand the reasons for the establishment of the alert force in order to believe in what you are doing and, consequently, do it with all your heart and to the best of your ability.

We no longer have a monopoly in nuclear weapons and long-range bombers. Many of the rapid advances in military technology which are reflected in our weapon systems are also utilized by the Soviets, permitting them to attack us with greater speed, firepower, and accuracy. . . . We received a form of strategic warning of communist aggression as early as 1848 when Karl Marx and Friedrich Engels published the *Communist Manifesto*. Ever since, all the top men of the communist hierarchy—from Lenin to Stalin to Khrushchev—have made it clear that the ultimate goal of communism is the liquidation of the capitalist countries and, primarily, of the United States.

It is my considered opinion that a combat-ready alert force of adequate size is the very backbone of our deterrent posture. Maintaining as much as one-third of our strike forces on continuous alert will not be easy, but it can and must be done. The success of this system depends on you, and I count on you to insure that the alert force will always be ready to achieve its vital objectives.

Thirty-four years later, on 28 September 1991, Gen George L. Butler, CINCSAC, broadcast a message to the SAC alert forces. That message read, in part, "It is clearly one of the singular events of our time that . . . I sit here in my command center. . . . I see all of SAC's bomber forces off alert. Today we especially salute the men and women of the Minuteman II force. Their contribution to this mission has now been achieved and they can stand down from alert with enormous pride and the gratitude of the entire nation, indeed of the entire world. This is a great day for SAC. It's [a] sweeping tribute to 45 years of unparalleled devotion along with our brothers in the SLBM force. We can sit quietly and reflect on the wondrous news that we've begun to climb back down the ladder of nuclear confrontation."

At the heart of the long period of US success in maintaining deterrence against Soviet aggression was a compelling national will, great leadership, innovative technologies, a superior industrial base, and, most importantly, young American men and women willing and able to meet the challenge. The United States clearly enjoyed the unsurpassed patriotism and loyalty of its Cold War military forces. They served, they trained hard, and they performed incredible missions without fanfare—and mostly without recognition. They worked long hours with short pay; their families sacrificed with them; weekdays blended with weekends; long absences from home were the norm rather than the exception;

yet morale remained at an amazingly high level. The discipline was exacting and their commitments were unsurpassed. The early Cold Warriors of the late 1940s and the 1950s grew into older Cold Warriors and senior commanders of the 1970s and 1980s. The strategic nuclear deterrent force of SAC and the submarine Navy became an even more elite professional war-fighting, war-capable "machine." *Peace was their profession*, and they maintained it.

Boomer Patrol Operations

Submariners have grown out of a tradition that's different from any other in the military. We go places on our own and come back on our own; we have a lot of adventures we can't talk about. Every submariner undergoes extensive screening, and most attend difficult schools to get here. All are volunteers. Even though our work is dangerous, we're not going to stand out as heroes. The submarine force attracts a different kind of sailor.

—A submarine commander

The Blue and Gold crews that man the SSBNs are among the Navy's *elite*, equaling the proud *Top Gun* fighter pilots. Like all nuclear Cold Warriors, the SSBN crews were all volunteers. Directed duty assignments to these jobs wouldn't work; desire and motivation must bring this special breed to serve aboard an ocean-submerged "operations center," cruising for months at a time, separated from families, and working within a cramped and stress-filled environment.

Privileged in 1981 to have a "dollar ride" aboard SSBN 641, the *Simon Bolivar*, I was able to observe virtually every "normal operations" activity aboard the submarine, including the simulated launch countdown of a Poseidon SLBM. My Navy deputy at joint strategic target planning staff (JSTPS), Capt Ernie Toupin, had to exercise very little persuasion to convince me to accept an invitation to fly down to Cape Kennedy for a Poseidon prelaunch checkout cruise. During the 24-hour "out to sea and back" ride, the executive officer gave me a hands-on tour of the boat. As we sailed out of the harbor to the dive area, I experienced a brief period of embarrassing nausea.

Having been involved in high- and low-altitude nuclear weapon release exercises aboard bombers and in Minuteman ICBM launch exercises, this adventure completed my indoctrination of weapons execution within the entire Triad. My impressions were as I had expected—exceptionally bright young professionals, officers and sailors, extremely courteous and polite (even during my nausea episode), and having positive attitudes, efficiently going through their procedures— no nonsense throughout. The launch exercise execution was flawless and impressive.

The next night, following my SSBN cruise, I went aboard the USS *Yellowstone* to observe the actual launch of the Poseidon—from the *Simon Bolivar*, which had returned to carry out the exercise. The missile breaking the water surface with a spectacular roar and fire from its first-stage engine was awesome in the predawn hours.

The men who signed up for SSBN duty were (and are) the cream of the crop. In addition to their personal motivation to serve aboard nuclear submarines, they are also exceptionally intelligent and physically fit. The average age of the enlisted nuclear submariner is 23 years. About half of them are married. The Navy began psychiatric studies in 1958 to determine the abilities of men to perform efficiently for periods of 60 days or more without personal contact with their families or the outside world. Capt (Dr.) Jack Kinsey, USN, concluded after cruising with SSBN crews that the key to a crew member's attitude and motivation to serve is training and discipline. The technical training is the most complex of any of the military services for a young high school graduate. The specially selected enlisted men train in four principal areas of study: electronics technician, fire control technician, missile technician, and torpedoman. Following "boot camp," or basic training, the SSBN candidates attend a technical school to train in their specialty for 38 to 45 weeks. They are expected to master electronics theory, mathematics, trigonometry, geometry, calculus, systems circuitry, test and diagnostic equipment operation, and normal and emergency operating procedures. Academic testing and hands-on laboratory evaluations are persistent.

Upon completion of basic technical training, the candidate attends submarine school for two or more months to become familiar with underwater seagoing operations. Thereafter, each crewman begins to concentrate on his specialty position within the SSBN crew. Training continues after he is assigned to either a Blue or Gold crew, and he does not win his *Dolphins Wings* until he is fully certified by the captain of his submarine. The captain of a crew—normally in the grade of commander and 38 to 40 years of age—provides leadership, training, and mission awareness to his crew of 140 to 200 men, depending on the particular submarine.

The captain remains constantly aware of the attitude and morale of the crew. A couple of hundred men working and living in a very small confined area can easily breed discontent if just one individual fails to adjust. Perhaps the most difficult living problem is the "hot bunking" requirement for the youngest and lowest-rated enlisted men. Depending on the number of "extras" on board, many of the younger sailors will be assigned three men to two sleeping bunks, or even two men to one bunk. Thus, one or two may be resting or sleeping while another is on duty. And the bunk space isn't all that "abundant" in the first place—roughly about a "roomy coffin" size, with a curtain to draw for darkness and privacy. Space for personal effects is also in short supply. (But who needs money or personal effects on patrol anyway?)

Duty shifts vary but are almost always four six-hour shifts or three eight-hour shifts per day. The division chiefs then assign duty requirements, training, and free time around the shift schedule. During patrols, most boats operate on "above surface" time—the "in-house" lights are all on during the day; dim red lights are switched on at night. This procedure also prevents night blindness, should the boat surface to use the periscope. The captain leans heavily on the other dozen or so officers and the senior noncommissioned officers to assist in creating a healthy living and operating environment.

Training is constant when the submarine is on patrol. Along with numerous functional exercises and drills, training helps to absorb the long hours and days at sea. The Navy, as did the

Air Force with the ICBM crews, offers college-level and vocational-technical courses to SSBN crew members. They study while at sea and take examinations when they return to their home port. The days and nights under water can also be absorbed with movies and video tapes if there is any time left after training, drills, and individual study.

But perhaps the favorite SSBN crew pastime is *eating*. The Navy spares no cost or innovation in providing the best in both quality and variety of food—and the cooks are arguably the most well-trained and most highly motivated the Navy can find. Of course, the "front end" of the patrol offers the best variety of fresh vegetables and fruits, with days toward the end moving toward frozen and canned provisions. The high-tech food industry, however, has created numerous innovative ways to preserve virtually every kind of food. A by-product of eating, of course, is weight gain—so the SSBN submarines carry a variety of exercise contraptions for the crew to use.

Every submariner looks forward to "word from home" during patrol, and the word is provided via "familygrams"—40-word messages limited to routine family news and events. The messages are screened at the home base for sensitive revelations, bad news, deaths, "Dear Johns," and so forth. Bad news must be kept until the sailor gets back home. Wives and family members become skilled in "packing" good news and information into the 40-word "grams." These messages are transmitted in the "open," on predetermined frequencies for the identified SSBN to intercept; thus, the submarine's position is not revealed. For the same reason, submarines on patrol are not permitted to transmit messages of any kind; therefore, crew members cannot send replies during the entire patrol.

The Soviets had an early lead in underwater war fighting, but rapid advances in submarine, nuclear propulsion, and ballistic missile technologies in the 1960s and 1970s pushed the United States far ahead and made the SSBN an integral part of the strategic nuclear deterrent force. The combination of stealth, mobility, survivability, endurance, and dedicated crews has given the United States an unequaled war-fighting capability.

Chapter 4

Fun, Games, and Serious Business

The Cold Warrior enjoyed a variety of fun, games, and serious business—quite often, a combination of all three. I will take only a brief excursion here to review a few of the events and circumstances that provided a continuous supply of "spice" to the otherwise challenging responsibilities of these Warriors.

Combat Crew Duty

This was at the core of the Cold Warrior's assignment and responsibilities. Becoming qualified in his crew position (pilot, navigator, bombardier, engineer, gunner, ICBM crew member) within the unit's weapon system (bomber, tanker, recce aircraft, ICBM, SSBN) was the Cold Warrior's initial step toward being assigned to a combat crew. Training usually began at a "school" for the appropriate aircraft or missile system, and was completed at the crew member's assigned unit. Once he had attained weapon system proficiency and was evaluated, usually in concert with the entire crew, the Cold Warrior began the certification process.

Every Strategic Air Command (SAC) combat crew member would likely argue that his type of duty was the most difficult and challenging, but most would agree that the bomber crew had the toughest series of requirements to meet in order to be "certified" combat-ready. In addition to being fully qualified in his aircraft position, the bomber crew member had to be fully knowledgeable about his single integrated operational plan (SIOP) mission plan: He was required to know the nuclear weapons that were assigned to his sortie and the tactics used to deliver them; the precise navigation route for entry and egress into his assigned target areas; the planned and emergency air refueling areas and tactics; the potential SAM and fighter threats along his route of flight; the escape and evasion plan if his aircraft were shot down; and the emergency airfields along his route of flight.

93

The crew member's certification briefing was given to a board of experts, including senior officers of the unit, who took great delight in challenging every facet of his knowledge. Most would agree that the certification process for the crews was every bit as comprehensive and challenging as preparing for an advanced college degree oral examination or defending a thesis. Failure meant embarrassment, back to the drawing board, many hours of study and preparation, and another try. Successful completion, on the other hand, meant "hallelujah," congratulations, and back-slapping. All SAC combat crews, regardless of assigned weapon system, went through the certification process.

An additional crew responsibility was participation in the human reliability program (HRP) and the personal reliability program (PRP). These programs sought to ensure that each combat crew member was mentally and psychologically fit to manage, handle, and employ nuclear weapons. In the early days of SAC, this was particularly important because many bombers could not make it to a preplanned poststrike base and the crews had to bail out of their aircraft sometime after dropping their last weapon. As longer-range bombers and increased air refueling became available, this problem all but went away.

I never saw or heard of a combat crew member asking to be relieved of his duties for lack of a plan to land safely after the mission. However, in the 1960s and 1970s, a few individuals who were selected for ICBM crew duty expressed reservations about launching missiles against an enemy. These incidents were relatively few in number, however, and in virtually every case the individual was reassigned without prejudice. *These activities were serious business!*

SAC Bombing Competition

Within SAC, flying always came first with the combat crews. Gen George C. Kenney, SAC's first commander, inaugurated the first "bombing competition" in 1948. During the first two years of its existence, the command's bomber crews had demonstrated very little skill in bombing accuracy. Kenney sought to improve both discipline and capability by organizing a "tournament" to create competition among the crews across SAC. The first competition was held from 20 to 27 June at Castle AFB, California, with ten B-29 bomb groups competing. During the competition, the crews flew identical navigation routes to predesignated targets, making three simulated visual bomb releases and three radar releases from 25,000 feet. 1Lt Merle J. Jones and his B-29 crew won the inaugural competition. (Later, Lt Col Merle J. Jones was my B-52G squadron commander.)

Gen Curtis E. LeMay took command of SAC on 19 October of that year, replacing General Kenney. He continued the competition the following year with three B-36, seven B-29, and two B-50 crews. From the outset, General LeMay imposed the requirement that combat crews would be fully "integral"; that is, every effort would be made to keep combat crews together as long as possible. They would train together, eat together, and fly together, thereby improving their coordination and proficiency. A B-36 crew won the second year's event. Now convinced that the bombing competition encouraged a competitive spirit, better proficiency, and improved morale, LeMay made the event an annual affair. Later, challenging navigation routes and electronic countermeasures were included. Still later, reconnaissance aircraft and crews were added to the event. Each year, as SAC grew and more sophisticated aircraft entered the inventory, unit competitions leading to the SAC-wide "tournament" became more spirited and challenging.

As a young B-36 pilot, I was fortunate to serve with a crew of the best professionals I was to ever fly with—and to be selected to participate in the Eighth Annual SAC Bombing-Navigation-Reconnaissance Competition at Loring AFB, Maine. The competition featured B-47, B-36, and B-52 bomber crews, along with RB-47 and RB-36 reconnaissance crews, in one of the largest competitions ever held. Our crew didn't win, but competing with the best combat crews and Cold Warriors in SAC had its own special reward.

Later, as the ICBMs came into SAC's nuclear inventory, missile competition for the crews was initiated. The first event took place in April 1967 at Vandenberg AFB, California, with two combat crews and one target alignment crew from each of six Minuteman wings and three Titan wings participating. Since the crews could not actually launch their missiles, "missile procedures trainers" (MPT) were used. Evaluators provided different emergency procedures for the crews to perform under different scenarios. The complex scenarios and emergency situations tested every facet of combat crew proficiency in maintaining and operating the systems. The missile competition served the same purpose as the aircraft competition program in building competitive spirit within and among the units, thereby enhancing crew proficiency. These were the "games," and they were "fun."

Spot Promotions

Following the second bombing competition in 1949, General LeMay decided to petition and "challenge" Headquarters Air Force to grant him the authority to award "spot promotions" to deserving, specially selected combat crew members who excelled in their performance. On 21 December 1949, the Air Force authorized SAC to "spot-promote" as many as 237 deserving first lieutenants to the rank of captain. Unit commanders nominated candidates; SAC headquarters made final selections. The spot-promoted captain held his rank until promoted through the normal selection process except when it was determined that he had failed to maintain the highest degree of proficiency and competence. In such an event, he could lose the promotion and revert to first lieutenant.

In 1950, the Air Force authorized SAC to spot-promote deserving officers serving on bomber combat crews one grade above the level they held (up to lieutenant colonel) and noncommissioned officers serving in crew positions (up to master sergeant). With the promotions came the increased pay and recognition of the new grade. SAC created a combat crew proficiency-level system: *Noncombat Ready, Ready, Lead, and Select.* A combat crew was upgraded from "lead status" to "select status" when one or more of the crew received a spot promotion.

The principal purpose of the spot promotion program was to reward exceptional performance by nuclear bomber crew members. Winning crews in the bombing competition or involvement in other exceptional events usually could expect to be rewarded with spot promotions. Also, loss of the spot promotion, by the entire crew or an individual crew member, could be expected if one or all failed to maintain the highest standard of performance.

I was one of the fortunate ones; I held a spot promotion for over two years before my normally scheduled promotion to captain came through. "Holding" a spot promotion probably induced more pressure on the individual and the crew than was recognized—one "screwup" by any crew member usually meant that all "went back to the real world." Pride and euphoria, however, glossed that over.

Needless to say, the spot promotion program was extremely unpopular with the rest of the Air Force, including the aerial refueling tanker crews within SAC. Likewise, the Navy had a legitimate argument on behalf of their SSBN crews. Nevertheless, General LeMay held forth and prevailed against the wave of criticism.

The Air Force terminated the spot promotion program on 30 June 1966, after 16½ years during which an untold number of SAC bomber crew members were rewarded for their exceptional performance under General LeMay's special reward program for the nuclear bomber force. This was part of the "fun"—at least for a few.

Combat Crew Proficiency

Maintaining individual and combat crew proficiency in carrying out the Cold War mission was a hallmark of Strategic Air Command. General LeMay set the early standard, and there was a continuing evolution of methods to test, check, evaluate, and "proof-test" combat crew, maintenance, and support personnel. At unit or wing level, the standardization-evaluation crews—the acknowledged best and most proficient crews in the organization—were selected to serve as the "standard setters" and evaluators. But internal evaluations were not the only means of assessing and determining combat crew proficiency; there was always a *higher order* in SAC. Bomber and tanker crews were periodically evaluated by the strategic evaluation squadron (SES) while ICBM crews were subjected to strategic missile evaluation squadron (SMES) evaluations. These combat crew specialists made scheduled visits to SAC units for the purpose of evaluating the local standardization-evaluation crews as well as several other crews selected at random from within the organization. Aircraft and missile maintenance teams did not escape the rigorous evaluation process either, as special higher headquarters evaluation teams also made periodic visits to units for evaluation purposes. This method, considered "onerous" by the crew force and the maintenance teams, did serve to balance standards and enhance performance across the entire command. Evaluations were not considered "fun," but "serious business" by most; they *were* challenging.

Operational Readiness Inspections

The most dreaded announcement within a SAC wing was, "The IG has landed!" The SAC Inspector General (IG) and his team of 40 to 60 inspectors would suddenly appear out of nowhere in his KC-135 tanker-transport and be on final approach to the base before anyone knew it. The speculation about when he would be coming almost became a "lottery event," which the IG Team usually won—sometimes by arriving in the dead hours of the night to "catch the unit unaware." Whereas combat crew performance evaluations assured crew proficiency, the "operational readiness inspection" (ORI) conducted by the IG was designed to evaluate the entire unit's ability to react upon receiving a no-notice alerting order to perform its war plan. The ORI was a rigorous inspection that usually lasted a week or more. The first event was to evaluate the response of the bomber and tanker alert force (or the ICBM force) to a simulated emergency war order. IG evaluators would be positioned at every conceivable location to witness and evaluate the response actions of both combat crews and support personnel.

The crews who happened to be on alert when the ORI was initiated were evaluated first. The entire wing was then required to "generate" the remainder of the bombers, tankers, or missiles up to full combat-ready status, with nuclear weapons loaded as if prepared to go to war. Again, evaluators were positioned to assess and evaluate response actions.

The entire organization worked in unison to demonstrate its capability to carry out the mission. Bomber and tanker wing crews, after downloading their aircraft from the fully generated war-fighting configuration, were then required to fly a simulated wartime mission over a predesignated route around the United States (with evaluators on board to monitor proficiency). Combat crew activities were not the only items of interest to the IG evaluators, however; all other facets of the unit's operations were also carefully inspected. Personnel, hospital dental clinic, commissary, base exchange, motor pool, day-care center, service clubs, and overall housekeeping records were carefully examined throughout the unit. Finally, everyone took a deep breath and headed for the base theater or auditorium for the *ORI Critique.* These formal presentations "laid out" the good, the bad, and the ugly of the unit's performance. Usually the commander of the unit's next higher headquarters would be present to hear the results. If it were going to be a "bad" critique, he would definitely be there—after all, he had to give an accounting to SAC. In fairness to the senior commanders, however, I should note that they attended as many ORI critiques and outbriefs as they could in order to congratulate the crews and personnel on the job well done. In the early days, it was not unusual for General LeMay to personally participate in the ORI, arriving even before the finish to observe the activities. He was also known on occasion to accompany the IG Team on their initial arrival. These were "games," but they were also "serious business."

Security Evaluations

Security awareness and safeguarding the nuclear-related and other war planning activities were a constant concern for every individual—and for commanders in particular. To stimulate consistent interest and awareness, SAC operated a security evaluation system. The system's two-phased approach utilized a specially trained team whose mission was to surreptitiously breach a unit's security measures. These teams used false identifications and false orders, picture badges with photos other than the wearers' photos inserted, and other creative schemes to "get inside" a secure area. (In some bizarre instances, picture badges bearing animal pictures got by the security guards. The ploys were all exercised in good faith and seldom ended in any serious consequences except for embarrassment and serious "lessons learned."

The second phase of these evaluations included complete audits of security procedures, inventories of classified materials, and tests (both oral and written) for personnel having responsibility for maintaining documents and/or systems security. The system seldom failed beyond an occasional administrative mishap. The SAC security forces at all levels were well-trained, indoctrinated, and disciplined. They were *elite* professionals, mostly very young enlisted men and women, who took their jobs as seriously as did any segment of the military. For three years, I occupied an office that was three floors below ground level at SAC headquarters. It was the most secure area in the entire building—perhaps in the world, since the area housed the US nuclear war planning activity, the Joint Strategic Target Planning Staff (JSTPS). In addition to the traditional closed-circuit television monitors and special-coded cipher locks, one had to be recognized by at least two manned guard stations on the way in.

One brutally cold Sunday morning, I received a call from the command center to come in and read a message that had just arrived. So I bundled up in civilian clothes, put on my fur-rimmed, Russian-looking hat, and proceeded to the office. At that time, SAC general officers assigned to headquarters staff were not required to wear picture identification badges since the unit's elite guards were required to personally recognize every general officer in SAC headquarters.

On that morning, my "disguise" was too good. I "breezed" by the guard station, said "good morning," and headed toward the cipher lock on my outer office door. Suddenly, I heard a loud "HALT!" Before I could turn around, I was spread-eagled, my hands high against the wall and my feet spread apart—and the security alarm was ringing. Then I heard the familiar trotting of other elite guards' "jack boots" coming down the passageway. When I was allowed to relax, I took off the ridiculous hat and was identified immediately by the embarrassed guard, who could not have felt worse than I. Next morning, I went to the SAC chief of staff, related the incident, and strongly recommended that even generals be required to wear personal identification badges. In short order, all were directed to get one and wear it in secure areas. This was "serious business."

Survival School

Every Air Force aviator and Navy tactical systems crewman goes through some type of survival training program. SAC had its own special brand, since all SIOP bomber missions and many tanker and reconnaissance missions would have flown over extremely hostile territory of the Soviet Union and the chances of having to bail out of an aircraft hit by their fighters or air defenses was great. The original SAC survival school was located at Stead AFB near Reno, Nevada. Later, the school was moved to an area near Spokane, Washington. Every SAC air crew member was required to attend. The Stead school was three weeks in length, the first two weeks consisting of classroom training and local demonstrations on how to survive in the general area where we likely might have had to bail out. The instructors were some of the toughest and uniquely bright young outdoorsmen I have ever seen, before or after. During the first two weeks of training, the student learned about the possible situations he might expect upon finding himself in a strange and hostile land. He might be heavily "radiated" from detonated nuclear weapons, have injured crewmen to care for, and be in great need of safe food and water.

For the last week of the course, each combat crew was "dropped off" as a single unit at distant dispersion points in the wilds of Squaw Valley, California, where they would attempt to evade the "enemy" and survive for five days. Only

101

minimal survival food was issued, and the student had only the things he carried on his person—except for the parachute that he had "bailed out" with. Instructors were always nearby, but they did not interfere unless a situation became life threatening, which it sometimes did. Several crew members from my wing, severely frost-bitten, lost a few toes during the course one year. Fortunately, most Cold Warriors never had to use their survival training; but the few reconnaissance guys who *did* encounter the "enemy" could attest to its value. This Cold Warrior activity could qualify as "fun and games" occasionally, but it was "serious business" all the time.

These are but a few of the challenges the Cold Warriors faced over their years of service. There were hundreds of others, always "taken in stride," each one developing a better person. Thus, the Cold Warrior could not only do his assigned Cold War job efficiently and professionally—he could also prepare for reentry into the civilian world, which he had spent a large part of his life to protect. Continuing with this theme, I want to relate some of the *true* adventures and recollections that several Cold Warriors passed on to me.

Anecdotes

Anecdotes, better known as "war stories" in the military vernacular, were an important part of Cold Warrior lore. These unpublished experiences served to enrich even further the Cold Warriors' lives. Not unlike a rumor, a war story tended to take on extraordinary embellishments as it circulated. Here, I simply pass on some of the anecdotes given to me by colleagues from the past—along with a few of my own.

I can think of no better way to begin than with General LeMay, the acknowledged "father" of SAC, who became a legend larger than himself during his Air Force career. Another legendary figure was Admiral Rickover, who enjoyed a reputation in the Submarine Navy not unlike that of LeMay in SAC. The accepted fact throughout SAC was that you could believe any story involving General LeMay, no matter how outrageous. The truth of the matter is that General LeMay is likely remembered more for things that he *allegedly* said rather than what he *actually* said. Likewise, the "spice" generated from encounters with Admiral Rickover made for interesting story telling. All who sought to enter nuclear submarine crew training dreaded the interview with the crusty admiral. Although the following stories were likely grounded in truth, some "gilding" was undoubtedly occurring as they were retold over and over.

General LeMay

Walter Boyne, in *Boeing B-52*, relates a story about General LeMay told by George Schairer, Boeing's Chief Aerodynamicist, during the early development days of the B-52 while Boeing was also attempting to "sell" improvements to extend the life of the B-47.

> Putting his arm around Shairer at a meeting at Boeing, General LeMay said, "*George, whatever you are doing to improve the B-47, stop it.*" But that wasn't sufficient for the eager Boeing engineers; Guy Townsend, test pilot for the B-47 and B-52, traveled to Omaha to brief LeMay on an improved B-47 powered by the J-57 engine. LeMay stopped the briefing before it got started by asking: "*Just how deep does a program have to be buried before you dumb sons-a-bitches at Wright Field will stop digging it up?*"

(The selling of the enhanced B-47 stopped and the B-52 got built.)

This author witnessed a similar event in November 1980. I grew up in SAC, in the "wake" of LeMay's great leadership, but I did not find myself in his presence except for a few times in his later years. On one such occasion, long after his retirement, General LeMay was visiting SAC headquarters at the invitation of Gen Richard Ellis, who was the CINC at the time. Having served as his executive assistant years before, General Ellis was always very comfortable with LeMay. The CINC invited four of us on the senior staff to meet with General LeMay in the "command conference room" to discuss current issues. General Ellis had intended to "try out" a new bomber program initiative on LeMay in this small group, hoping to get his nod of approval. But before we had all settled in our chairs, General Ellis was called out of the room to take an important phone call. In departing, he asked the vice CINC,

Lt Gen Dick Leavitt, to give LeMay a brief overview of a SAC proposal to radically modify the FB-111 bomber, making its capability similar to that of the B-1, which had been canceled by President Carter. The "fuse had been lighted!" When the first slide showed an FB-111 in flight, General LeMay slapped the conference table with the palm of his hand and said, "*Listen, you guys, Lyndon Johnson shoved that Texas-built F-111 up my a—once, and I'll be damned if I'll be a party to it a second time! What else do you want to talk about?*" (It seemed an eternity before any conversation resumed.)

As we know, President Reagan restored the B-1 program soon after his inauguration in 1981 and the FB-111 modification notion went no farther. The "Old Man" likely allowed himself to smile.

General Ellis related another LeMay story to me while we were waiting outside the Joint Chiefs of Staff conference room to brief the Secretary of Defense and the Joint Chiefs on the revised SIOP. Recalling General LeMay's reputation for "petrifying" briefing officers, Ellis told about a time when a young captain was scheduled to brief the legendary general. The captain was standing at the lectern when the "Boss" came into the room and took his seat. Several minutes elapsed while LeMay discussed various subjects with the staff around him. Meanwhile, the young briefing officer at the lectern had become "locked" in fear and "frozen" in his standing position, gripping the lectern for support. When General LeMay turned suddenly to the captain and said, "*Well what are **YOU** going to tell me?,*" the young briefer just "keeled forward," lectern and all, as he fell face-down on the carpet. The young captain was not injured, but his boss had to give the briefing.

General LeMay, reflecting on Korea in an interview with the Air Force Office of History, commented on how the United States elected *not* to use strategic weapons:

> Right at the start of the war, unofficially I slipped a message, *under the carpet,* in the Pentagon that we ought to turn SAC loose with incendiaries on some North Korean towns. The answer came back, under the carpet again, that there would be too many civilian casualties; we couldn't do anything like that. So we went over there and fought the war and eventually burned down every town in North Korea anyway, some way or another, and some in South Korea, too. We even burned down Pusan—an accident, but we burned it down

anyway. Over a period of three years or so, we killed off—what—twenty percent of the population of Korea as direct casualties of war, or from starvation or exposure? Over a period of three years, this seemed to be acceptable to everybody, but to kill a few people at the start right away, no, we can't seem to stomach that.

In retrospect, during the three years and one month of the Korean War, South Korea suffered 3,000,000 civilian and 225,000 military casualties out of a population of 20-plus million (16 percent); North Korea had 1,300,000 civilian and military casualties out of a population of 9,600,000 (13 percent).

Lt Gen Warren D. Johnson tells about an encounter he had with General LeMay. At the time, Johnson was a young officer assigned to SAC headquarters training division. SAC policy required that only officers with engineering or equivalent degrees be assigned to operate the intelligence collection hardware onboard RB-50 reconnaissance aircraft and to analyze the data collected.

After I flew several missions on the RB-50s to observe what they were doing, I became convinced that the six "recon" officers were overqualified and that well-trained enlisted personnel could accomplish the duties even better and far less expensively—and that they would enjoy much better job satisfaction. I visited the Training Command people at Keesler and they assured me that they could train a bright young enlisted man to do the job in six months. (The officers had been required to complete a one-year SAC-programmed course.) I went to my boss and in turn to the SAC Director of Operations, both of whom were not only reluctant to take the idea to the CINC, General LeMay, but were downright fearful of "rocking the boat." Finally, after a lengthy period of badgering, they both agreed to allow me to brief the general on my initiative—which they would attend, but *not* endorse the notion. I gave my briefing to General LeMay, who sat puffing his cigar, devoid of expression. When I finished, he said, "Who the hell's idea was this?" Both of my bosses looked blankly at each other as I finally gulped, "General, it was solely my idea." General LeMay paused for a very scary moment, then growled, "Best damned idea I've heard in five years. Do it."

Lt Gen Edgar S. Harris, Jr., former vice CINC of SAC and commander, Eighth Air Force, believed that General LeMay foresaw the impending nuclear era. He saw a need for SAC to implement unit-level possession of nuclear weapons. The old ways, he believed, would have to change dramatically. He therefore set out to bring about those changes. To convince

Congress that SAC should have its own assigned nuclear weapons in an airplane, ready to go by order of the president and not before, he knew there had to be an impeccable standard that SAC would have to hew to, and he set out to establish that standard. In other words, professionalism had to be introduced. In the doing of it, a number of people reputed to be LeMay's former associates, if not his friends, thought he was putting SAC under a constraint that was unreal—that it couldn't be done. They didn't fully subscribe to LeMay's demanding regimen. The proof of the general's grit lies in the fact that he held his position regardless of friend or foe, laying the groundwork for a "no nonsense" approach to professionalism. SAC achieved top-level professional standards that became accepted as such. "From that willy-nilly, harum-scarum, carefree, drink heavy, party heavy, be-a-good-guy-but [mentality] out of World War II (SAC moved) to the most professional and responsible fighting force ever assembled."

Admiral Rickover

Rear Adm Paul Tomb, a good friend and former colleague, tells the story about his first interview with Admiral Rickover. Tomb, a young lieutenant, was a nuclear submarine candidate. When the admiral referred to him as Lieutenant "Toom" at the outset of their meeting, Tomb corrected him: "Sir, it's 'Tomb,' like 'bomb.'" Admiral Rickover wasn't fazed and continued to call him "Toom." Finally, Rickover asked, "'Toom,' when did you first become interested in nuclear energy?" Lieutenant Tomb replied, "Sir, right after they dropped the atomic 'boom.'" Apparently, his reply didn't hurt his career; he got the nuclear submarine assignment, later became an SSBN crew commander, and finally retired as a rear admiral.

Another, *notorious*, Rickover interview occurred in 1959 when then Lt Comdr Elmo Zumwalt was a candidate for Rickover's nuclear submarine force. Norman Polmar and Thomas Allen, in *Rickover, Controversy and Genius*, discuss the interview in meticulous detail. Commander Zumwalt later became Admiral Zumwalt, chief of Naval Operations. Few, if any, written accounts of Rickover interviews exist; and although the admiral always kept a senior officer in the room as a witness, none have spoken publicly. The account of Zumwalt's interview, perhaps one of the more vicious ones, was recorded from his memory in precise detail and later made an official document. I will not repeat that interview here, but I commend to the reader the Polmar-Allen account.

Navy Capt Ernie Toupin, a member of my staff at JSTPS, told me the story of his "shakedown" cruise when he was first assigned to command a nuclear submarine. As was often the case in such shakedown cruises, Admiral Rickover elected to go out with him for a brief observation. Toupin was standing across the navigator's station from the admiral, trying to answer his "machine-gun-fire" questions while managing the submarine's onboard activities. Upon failing to hear all of one question, Toupin shouted back an answer but, as it turned out, *not the right one!* He looked up just in time to see a coffee cup sailing across the compartment at him, accompanied by a string of unmentionable expletives. The cup missed its target, but coffee covered the navigator's table and surrounding area.

The B-36

This great but ungainly bomber received its share of stories; many were respectful, some were not. Fresh out of B-36 ground school (there was no formal combat crew training squadron), I was scheduled for my "dollar ride" with one of the bomb wing's seasoned crews. I showed up at the appointed time and followed the pilots through their routines. They were polite, but not overly joyous about having a "tag along" on their mission—especially a second lieutenant who would only take up space—so I was mostly ignored throughout the process of last-minute planning, completing preflight procedures, and filing the flight plan.

Finally, as we were about to board the big monster, the aircraft commander summoned me over and told me to get aboard in the rear gunners' compartment. Sometime during the flight, he said, he would call for me to come forward to the main compartment "where the pilots hang out." The gunners, who were more polite, welcomed the "fledgling" to their "country" in the tail of the bomber. The next 24 hours were the *longest*—before or since—I ever spent in simply *waiting*. The "back end" troops took good care of me and the plentiful food was good, but the "call" to come forward never came. During the postmission debriefing, the aircraft commander finally acknowledged my presence. He timidly apologized for the treatment I had received, explaining that "they were awfully busy." And they *were* busy. But I vowed that day to make any "FNG" (fresh new guy) a special target of my attention whenever I was in a position to do so, no matter how busy I might be. Fortunately, this event was not the accepted rule in SAC, then or ever after.

Some years later, I was flying a B-36 that was forced to land at Davis-Monthan AFB, Arizona. We had a maintenance problem, and there was bad weather at our home base. The next morning, I went to base operations and asked for a vehicle and driver to take me out to my airplane, which was undergoing maintenance and parked at the far end of the airfield. As we approached the "magnesium monster," the young driver said, "Sir, which part of the airplane would like me to take you to?" I replied, "Just drive me down to number 6 engine where those guys are working."

Lt Gen Jim Edmundson, among his cherished accounts of the B-36, relates a story about the "bravado" of SAC's and General LeMay's penchant for air crew and SAC confidence building:

I launched in the lead plane [from Fairchild AFB, near Spokane] in a 15-ship effort at 4:00 a.m., climbed to altitude and headed for Davis-Monthan AFB in Tucson, Arizona. I picked up a block clearance from FAA and we established a bomber stream, using radar station-keeping with each B-36 tracking the airplane ahead of him and staying about one hundred feet above him and about a half-mile behind.

When we arrived in the Tucson area, I checked in with approach control and the tower for permission to land the flight at Davis-Monthan. I closed out our flight plan with FAA and set up a pattern to bring the flight in to land at 3-minute intervals. As each B-36 coming in on his final approach reached five hundred feet, the crew retracted the flaps, sucked-up the gear, poured on some power, and headed for Mexico at 500-feet altitude. We were on radio silence for the rest of the mission.

As far as FAA knew, we were on the ground at Davis-Monthan. SAC had placed a "trusted agent" in the tower who knew what was going on. Sneaky bunch that we were, we were on our way. To avoid ADC (Air Defense Command) radar, we flew about three hundred miles into Mexico and then headed west. When we were about five hundred miles off the coast, we headed north, still in bomber stream and flying at one thousand feet. We headed northerly all day and were off the coast of Vancouver Island by about 10:00 that night. At that point, we lit up the jets, turned southeast toward the United States and began a max climb to forty thousand feet. We assumed a spread formation with radar station-keeping, remained under radio silence, and turned off our running lights.

When we began showing up on ADC radar screens, the operators were sure the Russians were coming. But SAC had also placed a "trusted agent" in the ADC Command Center who announced, "These are not Russians, they are B-36s; go see what you can do about it." When we hit our pre-IP, each B-36 pilot went after his assigned target. We hit Seattle, Bremerton (shipyards), Renton (Boeing Aircraft plant), Tacoma, Portland, and a lot of other places. Our lead crew bombed Hanford (nuclear weapons components plant) and, after "bombs away," I told everyone to turn on their lights and contacted FAA for clearance to descend and fly back to Fairchild. It was a pretty good mission. We hit all of our targets and nobody laid a glove on us. ADC was mad as hell, but I'm sure General LeMay was chuckling. He'd found out what he wanted to know about one of his units.

SAC Missiles

The late Gen Jack Catton, who grew up in SAC bombers and was once my Air Division commander, told a story about his first exposure to SAC ICBMs:

Think about this for a moment. I remember when General LeMay pulled me into the headquarters the second time to do requirements, and I got my first briefing on something called Atlas. "Christ," I had come from the 43d Bomb Wing, and we were still working real, real hard to bring our celestial navigation CEP (circular error probable—bombing accuracy) down, so that we would be sure of a good radar fix, and hit the target—all that good stuff. These idiots pulled me down into the basement (SAC underground secure planning center) and started explaining to me that we were going to shoot this rocket, that [it] was going to go five thousand miles and it was going to be within—what the hell did we have then—I guess a *mile* of the target!

Col John Moser tells a story from his days as a Minuteman crew commander:

Life on a SAC missile crew was constant study, reading tech orders and Emergency War Order procedures, training, testing, evaluations, and alert. The routine became so "routine" because the pressure was never off. The crew commander was ultimately responsible for how his crew performed and since this was my first command, I took it seriously. Not only were we tested back at our base, we were often given surprise evaluations by visiting staff members while we were on alert.

Our wing commander had a reputation for, one, being a living terror and, two, making surprise visits to launch control centers (LCC) to "look in on the troops." My crew was on alert once when the topside security chief notified me that the commander was on site and requested permission to come down to the LCC. Did I have a choice? After he entered the LCC, I gave him the typical visitor's briefing and he began to "poke" around the capsule. As luck would have it, a practice emergency war order came over the SAC "primary alerting system" at that time. My deputy and I proceeded to run our checklists, coordinate our actions with higher headquarters, and complete the exercise—in a *very* efficient and professional manner, or so we thought—and the commander departed without further comment. Upon arriving back at the squadron the next day, we discovered that we had *failed* the observed exercise. The commander had found a loose bolt lying under one of the electronics cabinets which, in his opinion, would have caused the LCC to not be "hardened" against a possible nuclear strike—that is, the bolt *could have* ricocheted around the capsule, possibly neutralizing our launch capability. The bolt probably had been there since the LCC was installed years before; however, forgiveness *was not* SAC policy.

Col Larry Hasbrouck, a former Minuteman combat crew commander and, later, a missile wing director of operations when SAC was under increasing pressure to allow female officers to serve on ICBM combat crews, tells this story: "I got a call from the wing commander. He said to take Capt Rex Stone (a missile combat crew commander) and his wife, Becky (an Air Force captain stationed on the base), to a launch control center. Have her go through as many weapon system checklist procedures as possible and report back how well she did. We did it. Becky followed the checklists, with her husband answering questions but not providing assistance in any way. She encountered no problem with the eight-ton blast entry door or the elevator. She had no problem with the inspections, and she did a great job with the 'touch and tell' launch procedures. When I called the wing commander back, I said, 'Sir, I know the people at SAC [who had called him] want you to tell them that she failed miserably, but she didn't!'" (Soon thereafter, women were fully integrated into the ICBM force—both Minuteman and Titan.)

Nuclear Weapons

"Care and feeding" of nuclear weapons became an integral part of early SAC combat crew operations. When the Air Force dropped the devices on Japan, the flight crew included a Los Alamos scientist aboard each B-29 to monitor the bombs and insert the critical core components before the bombs were released. After SAC assumed responsibility for strategic operations with atomic bombs, it was obviously not feasible to have a scientist assigned to each combat crew. Designated crew members were therefore trained as bomb teams within their assigned integral crews—first the B-29 crews, then B-50 crews, and finally B-36 crews. The aircraft commander, the pilot, and the radar-bombardier usually comprised the "special weapons team."

The early weapons designed for delivery by SAC bombers were modifications of the *Fatman* implosion device that was dropped on Hiroshima. The Mark-4, Mark-6, Mod-4, and Mod-5 were large, ugly, fat bombs. Each carried a uranium spherical cavity called the "pit," which was surrounded by shaped blocks of conventional high-explosive material. To prepare the bomb for release, the bomber had to descend to 10,000 feet or below, so one of the bomb team members could enter the nonpressurized bomb bay and insert a small solid ball—the "core"—into the pit. The core was attached to a cone-shaped extension mechanism and stored aboard the bomber in a carrying rack called the "bird cage." The bomb team member removed the core from the bird cage and inserted it into the nose of the weapon, screwing it into precision threads that placed it at the exact center of the pit.

The bomb team member then armed the weapon by removing safety "plugs" from the top of the weapon and inserting arming plugs that completed the electrical circuits when the weapon was released. An arming wire or lanyard closed the necessary circuits upon release, activating the batteries within the bomb. The weapon would then be prepared to detonate when its electrical timer ran down to a predesignated time or upon impact with the ground, whichever came first. These were not necessarily complex procedures; but during the early years of atomic weapon operations, the bomb team members had to be proficient in the complex details of weapon design, operation, onboard monitoring, and the core insertion/arming procedures.

All bomb team members took this training in stride, though most were neither engineers nor physicists; in fact, few had any kind of scientific background other than some college science or engineering courses. Proficiency came quickly, however, and we took the training quite seriously—we became "experts" in the "mechanics" of atomic weapon operation, monitoring, and safety. The detailed and explicit training included reproducing, from memory, drawings and schematics of the weapons' fusing and firing mechanism, the T-Box monitoring devices, and the arming and fusing sequences. Zero-error tolerance was required on all examinations and practical exercises. (Holding only a basic accounting degree, I eventually became a nuclear weapons instructor and evaluator—in addition to my duties as a combat crew bomber pilot.)

With the advent of thermonuclear (TN) weapons, "care and feeding" became much simpler for the combat crews. The TN weapons were wholly self-contained—no mechanical preparations by the combat crew were required. ICBM combat crews also became free of such responsibilities, other than routine electronic monitoring.

Entering the bomb bay of an in-flight bomber was never "routine"; conducting tedious operations while working in that precarious environment often tested both skill and nerve. When the B-36 bombers were being retired in 1958, their nuclear weapons had to be ferried from local base storage to a weapons depot at Manzano Base, near Albuquerque. The logical way to haul them back was in the bomb bays of the bomber that had been carrying them. One crew (I will omit the names) was tasked to ferry an MK-17 nuclear bomb to Manzano. The MK-17 was the largest thermonuclear bomb ever built for air delivery— 40,000 lbs. The flight, a brief 40 minutes or so from El Paso to Albuquerque, could be very turbulent on a hot summer day over the desert. Under normal operating procedures, safety pins were inserted in the bomb release mechanism while the

B-36 was still on the ground. The radar-navigator removed the pins after takeoff and reinserted them just prior to landing. The purpose of the safety pins was to preclude accidental release during takeoff or landing.

On this fateful day, everything was working great. The flight up the valley to Kirtland Air Force Base (off-load point) was hot and extremely bumpy. As the pilot prepared to enter the traffic pattern to set up his landing approach, he directed the radar-navigator to go into the bomb bay and insert the safety pins. The bomb bay housed a maze of cables, wires, fuel, hydraulic lines, and "you name it." All cables relating to the bomb release mechanism were enclosed in metal tubes that were clearly marked **"NO HAND HOLD."** As the radar-navigator was maneuvering to insert the pins, the aircraft was bouncing and hitting abrupt ground thermal bumps at two thousand feet down the traffic pattern. One severe bounce caused him to "grab something" to keep from falling onto the bomb bay doors. Unfortunately, "something" was the **"NO HAND HOLD"** cable tube that controlled the manual bomb release mechanism. Suddenly, the 40,000-lb nuclear bomb exited through the bomb bay doors and plowed into the desert below. One can only imagine the thoughts that reeled through the minds and hearts of that crew—especially the poor radar-nav who was hanging onto the cable tube and looking through shattered bomb bay doors at the ground below.

But there's more to this event and story: The bomb worked perfectly! It did not detonate because it had not been armed. The incident proved to be a testimonial for, and a great tribute to, the ingenuity and skill that designed, engineered, and developed the bomb's built-in safety features. Years later, I flew a B-52 mission with that same radar-navigator; we had a brief—but sobering—chuckle about the incident that could have created a new "Grand Canyon" in New Mexico.

Cold War Operations

Lt Gen E. G. "Buck" Shuler Jr, former commander of Eighth Air Force, relates a story about training and operational reality during the Cold War:

One unique mission experience occurred during Sky Shield II (SAC bomber exercise) in 1961, where for 24 hours, every civil and commercial aircraft stood-down so that SAC and ADC could practice their war missions. I recall that we launched eight B-52s from Carswell AFB in a MITO, practiced our "safe passage" procedures, and flew to a point just north of Hudson Bay where we refueled with eight KC-135s in cell formation and then turned south to act as Soviet penetrators so ADC fighters could run intercepts against us. We descended to low level over Lake Superior and made our bomb run against K. I. Sawyer AFB at 500 feet altitude and then, still flying at low level, attacked our second target, an Army Nike site at South Bend, Indiana. Can you imagine grounding all civil aircraft in this day and time so the military could practice their wartime mission?

Col John Moser, from whom we heard a story about his days as a missile crew commander, now tells a story from his days as a KC-135 tanker-navigator. He was sitting at home baby-sitting two of his children on an October day in 1962 when a call from his squadron operations officer instructed him to report to the squadron immediately—no questions asked. He left a note on the door for his wife, took the kids to a neighbor, and drove to the squadron headquarters. He and the other air crew members assembled in the briefing room were informed that they would be departing as soon as their aircraft were ready. Further, no one could make any outside phone calls. After they took off, they were able to hear President John Kennedy's declaration about the Soviets' intention to place nuclear IRBMs in Cuba.

Landing at Moron in the early morning, we were confronted with B-47 crews in a 'live aboard' posture with power carts connected to their aircraft and lunch wagons nearby. We all assumed SAC was in DEFCON 2. Then it really sunk in that we may be going to war. We went into crew rest, our tankers were loaded with fuel and generated to alert, and our missions began. Most days we flew two missions a day—refueling the incoming airborne alert B-52s over the Mediterranean as they proceeded to their alert patterns off the coast of the Soviet Union. After the third day, we were advised that our families had been notified of our whereabouts. As with all SAC warriors, we took the sudden disruptions in stride. I can't recall another event in my 30-year career when there was as much professionalism demonstrated as I witnessed during that crisis period.

Case in point was a refueling we had one night in the worst weather for that type operation that I had ever flown in. The visibility was *zero* at our refueling altitude. Under any other circumstances, the mission would have been scrubbed, but our designated B-52 was inbound and required fuel to complete its airborne alert mission. I picked up the bomber's beacon and gave him the weather situation; he proceeded toward our rendezvous point. The rendezvous was as perfect as any I had ever seen—neither aircraft ever had visual contact with the other until the bomber 'slid' neatly in under the rear of the tanker at 50 feet and got ready to connect with the tanker boom for his fuel. I was convinced that night that if the electronics worked properly, we could rendezvous and refuel in *any* weather condition. I gave great tribute to the B-52 crew for their skill in completing the maneuver; they had already been airborne for 12–14 hours, and had at least that much longer to fly—yet they were as fresh and alert as could be. SAC training and professionalism paid off again and again throughout that critical crisis period.

General Johnson, then a colonel, was commander of the SAC contingent at Sidi Slimane, Morocco, at the onset of the Cuban Crisis: "Sidi had 21 B-47s on alert, ready to launch against the Soviet Union. In the most dramatic period, when the United States was about to intercept the Soviet ships transporting the missiles to Cuba, I was in the control tower when two Russian MiG-15s suddenly came roaring down our runway. Before I could react, the MiGs were gone. I discovered later that an American fighter pilot flying out of a base in Europe had buzzed Meknes Air Base earlier in the day where the Russians were training Moroccan pilots!" (Gentlemen warriors are a courtly part of history.)

A story reflecting the intensity of the Cold War days among the combat crews and their families was passed on from an old friend who is credible to the core but wishes to remain anonymous.

The lives of SAC air crews were burdened with stress-filled routines of training, flying, exercises, SIOP target study, and alert duty. There was very little a crew member could take home and discuss with his wife, especially anything related to his highly classified SIOP mission planning. At a remote SAC base once, a gala party was ongoing at the officers' club and the band was playing loudly, when over the din of noise a wife was heard to yell to another: *'Why should you worry, my husband is assigned Moscow.'* The wing commander promptly had all doors to the club locked, stopped and dismissed the band, and ushered everyone into a room where he admonished husbands and wives alike for the apparent breach of security of very sensitive information. He then directed all of the officers to report to the wing planning office, called in the planners who were not present, and proceeded to reassign all SIOP targets. They all remained there for most of the night studying and certifying their new mission assignments.

Most who did not live the life of a Cold Warrior had no idea of the stress and the intensity that pervaded the depths of the Cold Warriors' lives. Col Al Lebsack, former B-36 combat crew flight engineer and, later, SIOP plans officer, reflects on Cold War stress:

> Stress during the Cold War was caused by the physical, mental, and continuous pressure of knowing and having to process Top Secret information as a daily way of life. The stress was worry; knowing that just one slip of the lip could cause career damage to oneself, or even worse, physical harm to the Country. For me, it was hard to leave my work in the office and comfortably visit with friends and family members—I was never at ease around anyone if they tried to discuss my job, war plans, combat crew duty, or any probing of my work in the military. The situation never improved. More responsibilities assumed greater stress. In 1956, as the wing performance officer with some 60 to 80 different SIOP targets and routes assigned to me—just knowing that bomber fuel loads, mission profiles and the assigned combat crew proficiency were the differences between success and failure if a mission were actually executed. Crews placed their lives on the line based on my planning accuracy. Knowing that fuel reserves were always at bare minimums, and that to reach the target, deliver the weapons and reach the recovery base was never a positive thought. My concern for the combat crew was always present in every facet of my calculations. Why more individuals associated with the SIOP daily did not become mental casualties, I'll never know.

Lt Gen Dick Burpee tells a story about Soviet Marshal Sergei Akhromeyev's visit to the SAC bomber and missile units at Ellsworth AFB, South Dakota, in 1988. General Burpee was commander of Fifteenth Air Force, and the chairman of the Joint Chiefs had asked him to host Marshal Akhromeyev's visit.

> The marshal was impressed with the air and missile crews. He asked a B-52 pilot his thoughts about dropping nuclear weapons on the Soviet Union. The young captain thought for a minute and said, "*I understand your question and the impact it would have on your country and the innocent women and children, but you should know that if the President of the United States directed me to bomb your country, I would do it!*" The Marshall only smiled. Later, he was introduced to a young missile officer, 1st Lt Jill E. Nagel, who accompanied him and his delegation into a *Minuteman* training simulator. Throughout the orientation, she answered all of his questions with superb professionalism. The Marshall asked her how she felt about having a nuclear missile fired at the Soviet Union. She replied: "*My job is to maintain the missiles and make sure they will fire on demand; and Marshall, I want to assure you the missiles at Ellsworth Air Force Base will do it.*"

116

The Cold War

Communism got a foothold wherever there was a poor economic situation—and the enemy became those with everything. As soon as a populace begins to realize they are never going to get all they need or want, capitalism (democracy) begins to get a foothold. Many years ago, an old Spaniard commented to me that the way for the United States to win the Cold War was to send a flight of bombers over the Soviet Union and drop nothing but Sears-Roebuck catalogs. When the Soviets got evidence of the choices available to democratic peoples, they would opt for our system.

—Vice Admiral Jerry Miller, US Navy, Retired,
former vice director, JSTPS

My overriding memory of my Cold War years in SAC is the great cadre of professionals who made the system work. It was truly a privilege to be associated with them. In retrospect, I find it almost incredible that such a group could have been put together and maintained without the need of the coercion of conscription. And, truly I think, they served out of love for their country and the conviction they were essential to its survival. God knows they didn't do it for the money (of which there was often very little) or for the easy life (which they didn't have). The work was hard, the life demanding, the rewards other than personal satisfaction, few and far between. Separation from family by alerts, TDYs, short duty tours, and so forth, went with the territory, but that didn't make them easy to take. But I loved it, I'm proud I did it, and I'd do it again if the good Lord would give me the chance. I really believe that what we did was crucial for the nation; and that we did it with an elan that would have made Jeb Stuart proud. Our country is better, and perhaps even exists, because we passed this way. I love my country without reservation and consider it the highest of all honors that I had the opportunity to serve her in a time of need. I think all true Cold Warriors feel exactly the same way!

—Brigadier General Bill Brooksher, USAF,
Retired, Cold Warrior

117

(The awesome and enduring massive power and presence of the US strategic nuclear forces kept the Soviet regime in check for the whole of the Cold War.)

They Also Served

In conducting research for this project, I attempted to derive a measure of thought and reflection from the wives of the Cold Warriors; they were the most reluctant participants with whom I talked. Of them, however, it can truly be said, *they also served!* It was common knowledge throughout SAC and the submarine Navy—indeed, throughout all the fighting forces—that the greatest burdens of the Cold War often fell on the wives and families of the Cold Warriors. The combat crews and the support personnel seemed to *always* be away when they were needed most.

Almost all the wives did finally agree to discuss their experiences, with most pointing to the Cuban Crisis as the most frightening period of their lives. Most combat crewmen were put on alert with their weapons systems, and many were literally moved out immediately to forward bases and overseas locations, forbidden to tell their families where they were going or when they would return. Some did not hear from husbands for weeks after their departure. The "war of nerves" that pervaded the country only added to their fear and concern.

I was flying B-52Gs out of Ramey AFB, Puerto Rico, when the Cuban event began to unravel. We increased our Chrome-dome airborne alert sorties and were either in the air or on ground-alert with our bombers fully generated and ready to launch. The consequences of the situation, unquestioned among the crew force, did not fully impact the families until the Air Force casualty assistance people began collecting personal affairs information and requesting each family to pack for immediate evacuation if necessary.

I was amazed, as were others who have told me since, that there was no panic among the wives and children—they simply went about their necessary preparations, just in case. *Rumors*, of course, were always a part of the Cold Warriors' lives and the lives of their families—especially during that tense period.

Many wives participated in support groups, led by other wives, that were very beneficial in providing counsel and comfort when husbands were away, when rumors were "flying," or when an accident happened. Someone once said, "The Air Force always gets two for the price of one." Only one spouse gets paid for serving, but *both* clearly serve.

This holds equally true for the other military services as well. The families of the SSBN crews endured great frustration and maintained great patience as their husbands and fathers went on their underwater patrols for "months" without any word to or from their families.

This has been but a brief acknowledgment of that special group of silent and unsung Cold Warriors—the wives and families—who carried out perhaps the most difficult responsibilities of all.

Chapter 5

Beyond the Call

Strategic Air Command's (SAC) last training mission for the Cold War flew on 31 May 1992. On that day, SAC stood down. The command and its hundreds of thousands of assigned people over the years had served their country and the Free World very well—global peace had been maintained for all. SAC's nuclear delivery systems and combat crews were distributed to other operational and reoriented commands within the Air Force. The strategic bombers were reassigned to the new Air Combat Command, the ICBMs to Space Command, and the air refueling tankers to user commands as required. Out of SAC at Omaha, a new joint organization was formed—United States Strategic Command (USSTRATCOM). USSTRATCOM's primary mission was to plan the strategy and tactics of US strategic nuclear forces in the event of war, and to execute the plan if necessary.

The US Navy retained command and control of its SSBNs, with planning and execution also residing with USSTRATCOM. During the 46 years, 2 months, and 10 days of SAC's life, 2,638 combat crew fatalities were recorded. The record, however, does not include fatalities that could not be *officially* attributed to SAC operations due to the sensitivity of the missions at the time. These resulted principally from classified reconnaissance missions that, in time, will be declassified. Only then will proper recognition be given to those Cold War heroes and their families for their ultimate sacrifice. To recognize each individual whose heroism is so deserving would fill an entire book; I will therefore highlight only a few in this segment. In doing so, I join my former colleagues in offering the highest praise to all who remain on the honor roll of Cold Warriors.

One of the very first Cold Warrior heroic achievements occurred on 8 May 1954, when Capt Harold (Hal) Austin and his RB-47 crew (copilot Carl Holt and navigator Vance Heavlin) launched on a highly classified mission out of Fairford Air Base, United Kingdom. Their mission: Make a daring photographic overflight of Soviet air bases near

Murmansk to confirm/deny the reported existence of MiG-17 fighters at three Northern USSR bases.

Other RB-47 "feint" sorties had been flown around the periphery to get the Soviet ground radar controllers accustomed to foreign traffic in the region. On the day of the mission, three RB-47s launched and headed around Norway toward a "turn-in point" to Murmansk. At a predetermined point along the route, two of the RB-47s turned around and headed back to their home base, leaving the single reconnaissance aircraft and crew to proceed over the Soviet airfields. The lone RB-47 "coasted in" at 40,000 feet, considered safe from the Mig-15s known to be in the area. As the crew completed photographing the first two of six targeted airfields, three MiGs joined their formation in an obvious attempt to make a visual identification. Later into the flight, six additional MiGs joined the formation to "get a look at the RB." Identified as MiG-15s, they did not attempt any maneuvering at such a high altitude. By this time, the RB-47 crew had completed taking pictures of the next two airfields and the Soviets had confirmed the RB-47's identity. They had also launched six more fighters—this time MiG-17s, which had more than enough capability to out-maneuver the RB-47 and shoot it down. The MiG-17s immediately began firing at the reconnaissance aircraft, but without success. Meanwhile, copilot Holt began trying to get his thoroughly "cold-soaked" and malfunctioning 20-mm tail guns to fire. He finally coaxed the guns to fire a couple of bursts, causing the MiG pilots to back off. One of the braver Soviet pilots finally did make an extremely close firing pass, hitting the "RB" in the left wing and knocking out the intercom radio system. Captain Austin continued on his mission, taking photos of the remaining airfield targets. The MiGs continued to make firing passes at the "RB" until it was well out of Soviet territory, but they failed to make any further hits. The RB-47 crew, now low on fuel, managed to get back over the United Kingdom, where they "hooked up" with a KC-97 tanker and took on enough fuel to land at Fairford. According to the crew—who were invited back to Omaha to personally debrief General LeMay—the intelligence people were ecstatic with the Soviet airfield photographs, as well as one close-up of a MiG-17 making a close pass under the RB-47. General LeMay commented, "There are probably several openings today in [the Soviet] command positions there, since you were not shot down." The copilot said, with considerable innocence, "Sir, they were trying to shoot us down!" LeMay, in a typical response and without so much as a grin, said, "What did you think they would do, give you an ice cream cone?" After the debriefing, General LeMay quietly awarded two Distinguished Flying Crosses to each of the three crew members, commenting that he would award them the Silver Star except that he would have to go to Washington for approval and that would take "too much explaining." (Hal Austin and Carl Holt tell their story in the Spring 1995 *Daedalus Flyer*.)

Just a week before this daring flight, on 29 April 1954, two Royal Air Force crews, flying US-provided RB-45C aircraft, allegedly flew an even more provocative photoreconnaissance mission over Moscow and returned unscathed. These crews were among the more fortunate "recce" warriors.

On 28 April 1958, during a routine B-47 combat crew training mission out of Dyess AFB, Texas, one of the aircraft's engines exploded and caught fire. When the fire couldn't be extinguished, the pilot ordered the crew to bail out. The copilot, 1Lt James E. Obenauf, could not get his ejection seat to fire, so proceeded to climb down to the navigator's escape hatch where he could bail out manually. He found the instructor navigator, Maj Joseph Maxwell, unconscious. Obenauf tried to revive him so they could both escape the aircraft, but was unable to do so. Obenauf then climbed back into his copilot seat and brought the B-47 under control (the fire had extinguished itself). He then proceeded to descend and head back to Dyess. Sitting in the rear copilot seat, with the incredible wind lashing his face from the open cockpit, Obenauf landed the aircraft safely and saved Major Maxwell's life. (Obenauf almost lost his eyesight in the process, and his near-impossible feat provides another great example of professionalism, discipline, bravery, and airmanship not untypical of the Cold Warriors.)

The last year of the Eisenhower administration saw a considerable increase in airborne reconnaissance activity, designed to evaluate Soviet advances in both fighters and

ICBMs. The CIA, convinced that the Soviets were deploying long-range missiles at remote launch sites, petitioned the president for "one U-2 flight per month" to confirm their suspicions. Previous U-2 photographs had been impressive, providing evidence of Soviet activities in all categories.

Both the CIA and the Joint Chiefs assured Eisenhower that it would be "years" before the Soviets would have a shoot-down capability against the high-altitude U-2. Senator and presidential candidate John F. Kennedy was hammering away at his "missile gap" theme. The president, however, was convinced that the Soviets were not creating a "missile gap" and that he could avoid going to Congress for additional DOD funds in an election year. So, "just days before" the scheduled Paris Conference, which would be attended by Premier Nikita Khrushchev.

Gary Powers, a civilian Cold Warrior recruited from the Air Force by the CIA, was chosen to fly this "last" U-2 mission. He took off from Peshawar, Pakistan on 1 May 1960. He was scheduled to fly a circuitous route (to avoid known SAM sites) to Stalingrad, the Tyura Tam missile test facilities, nuclear power plants in the Ural Mountains, suspected ICBM site construction at Yurya, a known ICBM site at Plesetsk, submarine pens at Severodvinsk, and the naval base at Murmansk. He was to land at Bobo, Norway.

Powers was well along into his flight, 1,300 miles into Soviet territory, when he was hit by an SA-2 Fan Song antiaircraft missile. His altitude was never revealed, but he was probably flying at 70,000–80,000 feet. That Khrushchev was participating in the annual May Day celebration in Moscow when he received notification of the shoot-down was coincidental—and probably unfortunate for Gary Powers.

President Eisenhower was informed when Powers was overdue at Bobo, but US authorities were as yet unaware that he had been shot down. A brief game of "poker" then ensued. The Soviets set a trap by revealing only photographs of the wreckage; there was no mention of the pilot. The US position was that there had been an "unfortunate incident involving an errant navigation flight which strayed off course." Authorities in Washington believed Powers had been killed and the U-2 completely destroyed. They were "sure" that the timing explosives would have been armed when Powers ejected and the aircraft would have been completely destroyed. If true, the Soviets would be unable to disprove the US position.

As it turned out, Powers could not eject and the timing device did not destroy the equipment because of damage done to the U-2 when it was hit. He bailed out manually, fell freely until his pre-set timer opened his parachute at 15,000 feet, and was quickly captured upon landing. The Soviets now had "everything"—the U-2 spy plane and its pilot—but Khrushchev allowed Washington to continue creating its "story." When the Soviets did finally announce that the Soviets not only had the plane but also the pilot, Eisenhower promptly stepped forward and admitted the whole event. Taken "off-guard" by Eisenhower's admission, Khrushchev "played it back" as US arrogance and contempt.

The U-2 incident generated a few interesting sidebars, one of which was that Powers, while getting out of his parachute harness on the ground, saw another parachute descending not far away. He thought at first that it might be a missile booster stage; later, he guessed it probably was a hapless Soviet pilot who had been "in the chase" and had gotten caught in the barrage of SAMs that had been fired at the U-2. Another story, which was not revealed until 1996, concerns Igor Mentyukov, a Soviet pilot. Mentyukov reported to the Russian newspaper *Trud* that he had been sent aloft in an "unarmed" Sukoi Su-9 (Fishpot B) interceptor to locate and "ram" the U-2. He said he overtook the U-2 and "it got into (my) slipstream and its (the U-2's) wings fell off." He also said his story had been "covered up" by the Kremlin to avoid "weakening the faith" in the Soviets' air defense capabilities.

An RB-47 reconnaissance "ferret" mission flown on 1 July 1960 over the Barents Sea did not fare as well as did Hal Austin's earlier mission. Ferret missions were designed to fly along Soviet borders and collect electronic emissions from radars and communications transmitters. On this particular flight, commanded by Maj Willard G. Palm, the crew included Capt Bruce Olmstead (copilot), Capt John McKone (navigator), and three electronic specialists (Ravens): Maj Eugene E. Posa, Capt Dean B. Phillips, and Capt Oscar L. Goforth. The RB-47 crew took off from the United Kingdom and headed toward their surveillance area, skirting around Norway to the Barents

Sea and 50 miles off the northern coast of the Soviet Union. Just before 3:00 p.m., navigator McKone verified the aircraft's position at greater than 50 miles north of Svatis Nos, a prominent navigation landmark on the coast. At that point, copilot Olmstead sighted a MiG fighter off the right wing; but the MiG disappeared and the crew continued on their flight plan. Soon thereafter, Major Palm was surprised to see a MiG flying just 50 feet off his right wing. As Palm maneuvered his aircraft to provide some distance between himself and the MiG, the Soviet fighter pulled in behind the RB-47 and began firing. The first burst from the MiG's cannons hit two engines on the left wing, causing the "RB" to go into an uncontrollable flat spin. Unable to get the aircraft under control, Palm ordered the crew to bail out. Only Olmstead and McKone were able to successfully eject out of the aircraft, however. Major Palm apparently stayed with the aircraft in an attempt to give the Ravens time to safely escape and then land the RB-47 at sea. The flight was monitored by allied radar until it crashed two hundred miles off the Soviet coast. The Soviets recovered Major Palm's body and turned it over to United States authorities. The three Ravens were never found. McKone and Olmstead were rescued by the Soviets and charged with espionage (despite their having been 200 miles off the Soviet coast). They were released on 24 January 1961, after seven months in prison, on orders from Khrushchev. Their release was called a goodwill gesture to the newly inaugurated President Kennedy. Meanwhile, Gary Powers remained in a Soviet prison for more than a year afterward—until he was released in exchange for Col Rudolph Abel, a convicted espionage agent being held in the United States.

On 14 October 1962, Maj Richard S. Heyser, flew a SAC U-2 over Cuba and made the first photographs showing construction work on Soviet IRBM emplacements. Thereafter, U-2 reconnaissance flights over Cuba continued on a daily basis for two weeks—until 27 October, when Maj Rudolph Anderson was shot down by a Soviet-built antiaircraft missile. US radar controllers tracked Anderson's aircraft from the time it took off at McCoy AFB, Florida, until the moment it was shot down. Major Anderson was killed, his body strapped in the wreckage of the U-2. The Cubans held his remains until United Nations

Secretary-General U Thant made a personal appeal to Fidel Castro for their return.

These are but a few examples of Cold Warrior heroism in the face of a hostile enemy. In contrast with the Soviets, who fired upon US reconnaissance aircraft over international waters numerous times, North American Air Defense (NORAD) fighters never fired upon any Soviet aircraft despite their having made hundreds of flights along and over US and Canadian borders during the Cold War years. At least 75 US aviators were killed by the Soviets while conducting operational surveillance missions—mostly over international territories.

Following the Cuban Crisis, tensions remained high wherever US and Soviet military forces converged, particularly in Europe. On 10 March 1964, a US RB-66 reconnaissance aircraft was flying along the East German border on a photographic mission while being carefully radar-monitored by allied ground controllers. For reasons never fully explained, the pilot flew the RB-66 directly into East Germany instead of making a scheduled turn away from the border. The ground controllers tried to warn the crew of their navigation error, at first in coded messages and then in the clear—all to no avail. When the aircraft was approximately 16 miles inside East Germany, it was intercepted by a MiG fighter and promptly fired upon. Capt David Holland, recognizing that the aircraft was hit and severely damaged, ordered his navigator, Capt Melvin Kessler, and his electronics officer, Lt Harold Welch, to bail out. All three were picked up by the East Germans. The United States immediately initiated contacts to return the airmen, but the efforts were bluntly refused. Lieutenant Welch, who had suffered a broken leg and a broken arm, was released 11 days later. Eighteen days after the shoot-down, and after many charges and countercharges by US and Soviet officials, the remaining two crewmen were also released. The United States and its European allies had strong suspicions that the RB-66 had been *lured* over the border by false navigation signals (the Soviets had used this tactic before). Several US and allied aircraft were lost during the Cold War due to signal-spoofing and communications jamming by East German and Soviet controllers. At least 31 US reconnaissance aircraft were shot down by the Soviets during the Cold War, and several American crew members were never accounted for. More often than not, Soviet or related rescue vessels or teams were quick to respond to these downed aircraft locations; but there was always denial by the Soviets that any crew members survived unless there was a political or propaganda advantage in admitting their survival.

The US Navy suffered the worst submarine disaster in recorded history on 10 April 1963, when the nuclear-powered USS *Thresher* did not return from a test and evaluation dive with 129 personnel onboard. Although built on an attack submarine keel, *Thresher* was in fact a prototype for the Navy, which wanted a "killer" attack boat that would later serve as a more advanced SSBN. The *Thresher's* long cylindrical-teardrop hull was designed to enhance speed and maneuverability while submerged, and to create a quieter "glide" through the water to avoid detection.

The concept behind *Thresher* was to create the quietest submarine in the world that would also be the best "hunter" in the world. Her improved sonar "listening" system had over 1,000 transducers and hydrophones for longer range and more precise detection of other submarines and ships. The *Thresher* concept also called for larger personal space for the crew (although this was almost never achieved in submarines), easier and more simplified operating systems, weapons handling, and firing systems, and a revolutionary fresh-air generating system that would permit longer periods of deep submersion.

All of *Thresher's* "moving parts"—generators, pumps, engine drive shaft, and fluid circulating systems—were flexible-mounted to absorb vibration and noise. The major shortfall in this revolutionary submarine was in the mating and welding of her structural members and pipes, which had to withstand tremendous sustained pressures at great ocean depths. *Thresher* suffered several pipe failures under extreme pressure long before commissioning. After commissioning, she encountered eleven fires (six at sea and five in dry dock), ramming by a tug while in port, and electrical failures. Of her 625 days of life after commissioning, *Thresher* spent 406 days in port or dry dock due to various problems. *Thresher's* advanced technology was there, however, and the Navy's nuclear underwater force became an integral part of deterrence.

Thresher was under the command of Lt Comdr John W. Harvey and Lt Comdr Pat M. Garner when she departed Portsmouth, New Hampshire, Navy Yard for postoverhaul and further sea trials on 9 April 1963. The crew included 12 officers and 96 enlisted men. Also on board were four staff officer-observers and 17 civilians, for a total of 129 personnel. *Thresher* rendezvoused with the submarine rescue ship *Skylark,* which was to provide surface communications during the dive exercises; they would be *Thresher*'s final exercises.

There has been considerable speculation, but no complete agreement, regarding the actual circumstances surrounding the loss of *Thresher.* Five years later, the SSN *Scorpion* disappeared in the mid-Atlantic with 99 men on board, en route from its Mediterranean patrol back to Norfolk, Virginia. Despite these devastating losses, the Navy continued to develop its underwater stealth technology and improve its capabilities. The nuclear submarine fleet became a formidable Cold War first line of deterrence, completing over three thousand SSBN patrols without incident.

B-52 operations also produced their share of heroes, including prisoners of war in North Vietnam and fatalities during both training and combat missions. The first bombing mission by B-52s over Vietnam, which occurred on 18 June 1965, proved to be a disaster for SAC. Twenty-seven B-52Fs launched out of Guam to bomb Vietcong positions in South Vietnam. Two of the bombers collided in midair before reaching the target area. Both flight crews were lost, including Maj Gen William J. Crumm, commander of Third Air Division on Guam, who was serving as flight leader on the mission. Furthermore, the bombing mission was almost totally ineffective.

At the end of hostilities, however, SAC B-52s were credited with bringing North Vietnam to the negotiating table. Hundreds of other crew members were lost in bomber and tanker mishaps during the Cold War years—all giving their "last full measure of devotion" to their country.

There were two major mishaps involving Titan II missiles during the latter days of the strategic system. The first occurred at McConnell AFB, Kansas, on 24 August 1978, when the Stage I booster nitrogen tetroxide oxidizer began leaking in the silo. Two crew members were fatally injured, the

129

missile was severely damaged, and the civilian inhabitants in the surrounding area were evacuated from their homes. The second Titan II accident occurred on 18 September 1980 at Little Rock AFB, Arkansas, when leaking missile fuel caused an explosion in the ICBM silo. The launcher closure door was blown off the silo and the nuclear warhead was found several hundred yards from the site. Two crew members were fatally injured and the launch complex was totally destroyed. Although lives were lost, the nuclear system's safety features prevented what might have been a national disaster. Congressional hearings and a "Blue Ribbon" committee reviewed the accident and certified the Titan II weapon system safe and effective. These accidents point to the inherent dangers faced by all nuclear weapon systems Cold Warriors.

The Cold Warrior lived in a tense and often frightening universe all its own. It was an environment that most people—the very people who were being protected—could never know. The Cold Warriors lived in alert facilities, missile silos, submarines beneath the oceans, and bombers in the air. They were seldom at home with their families or enjoying the recreational activities their civilian peers were enjoying. Often, there were political and/or media reactions to the great expenditures required to maintain our awesome weapon systems. Some argued that the money would be better spent for social services. One could easily counter this argument, however, by pointing out that a nation can give no greater social service to its people than their security.

Many citizens never really grasped the gravity of the Cold War; they were not personally touched by it, and they were never aware of the persistent dangers posed by our Cold War enemies. But the wives and families of the Cold Warriors understood.

Chapter 6

The Soviet Cold Warrior

The world surrounding the Soviet Cold Warrior was far different from that of his counterpart in the United States and the Western world. Since tensions began to relax in the 1980s, a great deal of information has accumulated about the Soviet military and the Soviet people, and about the harsh conditions they endured behind the now tattered Iron Curtain. The information has come mostly in the form of books and documentaries by Russian authors, some written during the Cold War, some written after the "thaw." Other information has come from "internal" documents developed for consumption by the Soviet military and from Russian newspaper and magazine articles. Many of these fall into the category of heavy propaganda. Only in very recent years have the more critical reviews been released.

Even at their very best, the Soviets' military forces were the "Achilles' heel" of the empire. Manning and maintaining a standing military force has been difficult in Russia over the ages, in great part due to persistent policies of forced conscription. From the early days of the Mongol enslavement, through the tsars and the communists, soldiers were forced into service and treated as chattel. Officers, on the other hand, were appointed by the governing entity—more often than not, from the aristocracy. Training came in the form of forced duty, forced labor, and severe discipline. From the beginning, Russian soldiers were conscripted from the peasantry. Poorly educated, they were accustomed to living and working in mostly undesirable circumstances. Prior to Peter the Great, Russian soldiers were mustered into service for a particular campaign, then released back to their former life.

After Peter the Great created Russia's first standing army, soldiers and sailors were forced into service virtually for life—or for death! Most never returned to their homes, many dying from disease rather than a bullet. Those who did survive to return home, having been released because they were of no further use, might find their homes and families gone.

"Ghosts" of the past, they were usually not welcome because they represented a further burden to the community.

Always unpopular in Russia, military service became even more unpopular under Soviet rule. Men and boys eligible for conscription often fled their homes and hid until they were found—or were turned in by a neighbor for a reward. Self-mutilation found its way into the twentieth century as potential conscripts cut off fingers, damaged eyes, or severely damaged a foot. After conscription, desertion was a persistent problem—until the later years, when the KGB and the border guards allowed few to escape. And deserters were subjected to brutal punishment, which was almost always carried out in front of the deserter's assembled organization.

Lenin attempted to motivate service in the Red Army by imposing *military pedagogy*, "the science of communist education, training, and indoctrination of the Soviet soldier and the preparation of sub-units and ships for successful operations under the conditions of modern warfare." The purpose of military pedagogy was to quell unrest and dissatisfaction among the ranks by instilling patriotism and communist ideology into their drab lives. Therefore, political indoctrination became an integral part of Soviet military training. The communists determined that a standing military force would be necessary to both defend their paranoia and intimidate the rest of the world.

The Soviets created at least three programs designed to indoctrinate young men and women. The *Young Pioneers* program featured a weekly military indoctrination period in the public school curriculum. Students were taught the basic military crafts—map reading, marksmanship, and first aid. They participated in field trips and exercises conducted to give them practice in the learned skills. The official Young Pioneer handbook was the *Tovarishch*, which contained descriptions of Soviet military roles and missions along with photographs of Soviet military equipment, including tanks, aircraft, uniforms, and insignia. Young Pioneers also learned about Communist Party policies as well as policies of the Soviet Government, and were indoctrinated on the requirement for a strong military.

The second youth program created to influence Soviet youth was the *Komsomol*, or Young Communist League, which was aimed at young adolescents to both inspire patriotism and foster antagonism towards noncommunists. The program was generously filled with Marxist-Leninist ethics and communist "morality" designed to motivate the young Soviet male to properly present himself to the district Military Commissariat (draft board) when he reached the age of 18. The Komsomol also had a dark side—it encouraged spying on family members and neighbors. Komsomol youth were trained to report any activities, conversations, or correspondence that might be interpreted as anti-government.

The *Dosaaf*, the Volunteer Society of Cooperation with Army Aviation and the Fleet, was created in 1951 as a "defense-patriotic organization." The purpose of Dosaaf was to promote active cooperation for strengthening Soviet military capabilities and preparing workers to defend their homeland. At its peak, Dosaaf's membership was estimated at 80 million workers and students (over 14 years of age). Dosaaf was characterized in Soviet journals as a sportsmanship club, but its interests clearly lay in paramilitary activities, weapons handling, marksmanship, parachuting, light aircraft flying, and sailing. All students of fourteen years and older were expected to join Dosaaf, as were their teachers and administrators. Dosaaf had a direct tie to the Soviet military under the Law of Universal Military Obligation, which required "call-up" of civilian workers and youth for training as communicators, drivers, radio technicians, and so forth. Dosaaf paid particular attention to students who demonstrated interest in communist doctrine and military skills (as potential officers). The Soviets assigned a high priority to Dosaaf, always placing a four-star military officer at its head.

One would think that all the attention given to young Soviets would lead them to eagerly serve their country—that young patriots full of communist zeal would flock to the district commissariats when they became eligible. There is ample evidence, however, that none of these programs were effective and that young eligibles often had to be tracked down and forcibly sent off to boot camps. The likely reason is that the Soviets, in typical fashion, *out-propagandized* themselves with their elaborate preparation programs. When young Soviet men returned to their home villages after two or more years of conscripted service, they brought stories of abuse, severe punishments, and food deprivation. They had a general hatred for the communist military and a genuine fear that they might have to go back. Next we will review in more detail the reported ways of life for Soviet Cold Warriors.

The Conscript

Virtually every young male reaching age 18 in the Soviet Union could expect to be conscripted to serve for at least two years in one of the five branches of the military—Red Army (ground forces), Strategic Rocket Forces, Air Defense Forces, Air Force, or Navy. There was also the possibility of being drafted into one of the KGB activities—frontier border guards or internal security troops. If and when the conscript was discharged, his service was not necessarily finished. He took a new uniform home with him to keep ready for possible recall until he reached the age of 50. The Soviets, with paranoia as an integral part of their psyche, consistently planned their requirements far in excess of the demand. They were always planning for what they believed *might* be necessary.

A considerable part of the Soviets' paranoia, which dates back to the beginning of their harsh history, was punctuated by communist control over the 70 years of the twentieth century. The paranoia extended to their 22,500,000 square kilometers of territory—more than the United States, Western Europe, and China combined—which was always surrounded by potential "enemies." Therefore, the entire perimeter had to be patrolled in one form or another. The Cold War years served to intensify their requirements for more and more troops in uniform. Conscripts were brought from every corner of Russia and the Warsaw Pact countries—even many Jews were called up to serve in the various branches of the military. Thousands of "stragglers," picked up along bordering countries, suddenly found themselves in a remote Soviet "boot camp." During the tense years of the Cold War, there was a persistent suspicion in the west that Soviet soldiers were "ten feet tall." Soviet propaganda, the worldwide media, and a tightly closed society accounted to a large degree for these perceptions.

The world finally learned the truth, of course, as the great Soviet "war machine" ground to a halt. A cleverly developed US Army intelligence report of the early 1980s concluded, "Despite the fact that the Soviet Army projects itself as the best equipped, largest tactical and strategic military force in the world, Western analysts can now speculate whether the man of steel has entrails of straw." It goes on to say, "The Soviet military is a brutal insensitive world where the military ethos is still locked in the eighteenth and nineteenth centuries."

It has been estimated that prior to 1990, the Soviet military forces required a continuous influx (1.8 million annually) of young people, mostly boys, to keep the five military services and the KGB uniformed forces up to their desired strength. The "raw material," which included emigres and "strays," came from all parts of the Soviet bloc countries. Every district in the Soviet Union had an office of the military commissariat, which acted as a "draft board" for conscripting recruits. These offices maintained files on all male children, from birth to the age of 18, at which time they were eligible for conscription. The files also contained ethnic, social, political, health, and school records, along with character references and records of participation in the *Young Pioneers, Komsomol,* or the *Dosaaf.* At "roundup" time, all of the draft-eligible young men were "interviewed" by *pokupateli,* recruiters from the five military branches who came around annually to select recruits. The Air Force and the Strategic Rocket Forces were given first priority for the better educated, brighter, and politically motivated boys. The less educated and less intelligent—but physically healthy and strong—went to the Navy; the remainder went to the Army, the Border Troops, and so on.

The recruiters were always looking for officer candidates for their service branches. To reduce escape opportunities, recruits were almost always put aboard a waiting train immediately after they were assigned to a service branch. They would likely not return to their home area for the duration of their enlistment. As recruits completed their initial indoctrination and training, they were almost always stationed as far away from their home districts as possible. The only exceptions were those recruits specially selected for the Border Troops.

As within any culture in the world, however, even in the Soviet Union, recruits found ways to evade conscription. In addition to self-mutilation, which we referred to earlier, money and bartering were used to influence the local commissariat. Alcohol, food, and livestock were the most common bartering goods.

The young Soviet recruit all but lost his identity at boot camp. Stripped of his clothing and personal possessions, he was deloused, had his head shaved, and was issued an ill-fitting uniform. He was also required to sew white cloth strips on the inside neck of his shirts for daily cleanliness inspections. By now, he was probably wondering what happened to the "grand picture" that had been painted for him by the youth leaders in his school and in his district.

Once out of boot camp, the recruit began training for the type of duty he had been selected for. After he completed this specialized training, his two-year tour of duty began—three years if he was selected for the Navy or the Coastal Security Force. He would have little opportunity to leave his assigned base, meet girls, eat in a restaurant, or visit his family. Contributing to this austerity was the fact that most Soviet military installations were located in remote areas, far from urban developments. (Some American Cold Warriors thought of Minot, Grand Forks, and Holy Loch as "remote"!)

Also contributing to the Soviet conscript's unhappy life was inadequate compensation. Up to and through the 1980s, the conscript received R3.50 (3 Rubles, 50 Kopecs—equivalent to $6.50) per month. Since then, inflation has skyrocketed and it is difficult to make any sense of an estimated comparative rate. Conscripts were "guaranteed" ten days of leave time during their two years of service, but often no leave was ever granted. And even when leave was granted, the conscript usually could not go home because home was too far away, and he had no money for train fare.

Turmoil within Soviet enlisted ranks was a persistent source of concern, but it was kept secret by the strictest of security measures. Another source of unrest, beyond that already described, was the food provided to the troops. Riots were alleged to have broken out because the food provided was of the lowest quality and in inadequate quantities. Such riots almost always led to severe punishment for the instigators. Most of the food served at Soviet installations consisted of canned meat, canned fish, and hard bread. Very few fresh vegetables and/or fruits were served. Salt fish and salt pork were the usual winter staples, along with a watery porridge called "kasha." Even when food was available from a nearby village or farm, the men had no means to pay for it. Therefore, it was not unusual for Soviet soldiers to forage for food whenever such opportunities presented themselves. Virtually everyone in the Soviet Union smoked tobacco, and the young "GI" was no exception despite the fact that the cheapest Russian-made cigarettes were 50 Kopecs per package—one-seventh of a month's pay. Personal items (soap, shoe polish, toothpaste) also had to come out of their pay.

The lack of nourishing food was also thought to have debilitating effects, both physical and mental, on the Soviet fighting forces. Food deprivation has been prevalent in Russian armies over the centuries, apparently due to a simple lack of interest among Russia's military leaders. The consequences have been poor physical conditions, stomach disorders, persistent dental diseases, eye problems, and weight losses among the troops. Nor has the Russian military been exempt from problems due to alcohol abuse, which has historically transcended all walks of Russian life. The enterprising GI could always manufacture alcoholic drinks from variously available products. Coolants are particularly good sources for today's soldiers working around vehicles, tanks, or aircraft. Shoe polish spread on bread and left out in the sun was known to be a popular source for desperate soldiers. (Poisoning generated by these methods caused the deaths of many young soldiers.) Drug use and abuse was and is much less common because drugs are less available and more expensive. However, "anash" (hashish), and "plan" (an opium product) have always been available along the remote southern borders.

The Soviets maintained a strict policy of keeping military personnel separated from population areas and civilians, wherever possible. The policy only varied in diverse ethnic regions where GIs were given more freedom to interact with locals. Stalin established a "resettlement" program utilizing the military within diverse ethnic states as a "bonding of cultures" process. Marriage to ethnics was particularly encouraged in the Baltics and the southern tier (Moslem states) to promote pacification. A RAND study reported that the Soviets took special care to send conscripts from ethnic minorities as far away from their homes as possible to discourage them from deserting. They were less likely to be a problem if they were far from their families, and they would not be available to join in potential uprisings within their native cultures if they were far away. Just as the British used Sikhs for special security operations, the Soviets employed tough Kazakh soldiers within the internal police to maintain control over military troops. The RAND study noted that, whereas a Russian soldier would probably have difficulty in shooting a dissident female soldier, a Kazakh would not. This was the Soviet military manpower that made up the "ruthlessly efficient 'ten-foot tall' soldier-elitist" whom the Western Allies worried about throughout the Cold War years.

The Noncomissioned Officer

Only about one percent of Soviet conscripts reenlisted at the end of their first term. Many, however, remained conscripted because their unit had no replacements. NCOs in the Soviet military always remained in short supply due to low reenlistment rates. The result was a lack of experience moving up the ranks. The comparatively few NCOs found in Soviet military units were known to be tough, hardened characters who literally operated their own internal network and organization. They were generally feared by all, especially young recruits, and were left alone by officers. Their businesses included extortion as well as selling and bartering stolen goods, alcohol, and drugs. They were not good role models for aspiring young men who might have sought to remain in service. Most conscripts, reflecting their back-home culture, easily fell prey to the hardened NCOs or by "old hand" conscripts.

The new recruit was likely to find himself forced to exchange his newly issued uniform for a used one, or to perform degrading jobs. Usually, he learned to comply with the demands placed on him, including demands to turn over his meager pay in order to avoid persecution. Many became menservants and slaves; others bought their way through the ordeal, begging money from home and giving it to the thugs.

Even into the modern-day Cold War period, the Soviet military structure relates back to the dark ages. Training is minimal, and is always limited to the absolute essentials of the job to be performed. The caste system is dominant, and punishments are severe. There is little motivation to perform professionally. Conscripts are deprived of basic human treatment and living conditions. The quality of their lives is deplorable. It is likely that these factors account in no small measure for the extraordinary losses of Russian and, later, Soviet fighting men in wars of the past.

The Officer

The wide chasm between Soviet officers, NCOs, and conscripts dates back to the days of the Tsars. Due in part to the lack of a professional enlisted or NCO corps, the Soviet officer corps is far larger than would be considered necessary in most armies of the world. Young officers often find themselves serving in NCO positions, directly supervising conscripts. This situation leads to even more contempt among the young enlisted men; they are often essentially the same age as their supervising officers. Adding still more unrest, even the youngest officers enjoy a much better lifestyle than do the conscripts. The average Soviet lieutenant makes twenty times that of the average enlisted troop. The lieutenant also has unlimited privileges and access to all the vodka he can drink. Compared to the conscript, the lieutenant lives and eats like a king.

Soviet officer candidates were often recruited by the same methods and from the same sources as the conscripts. The officer candidate was either brighter, had better academic grades, had performed well in one of the propaganda prep schools, was the son of a bureaucrat, or was a fair-haired boy who had caught the eye of the district commissariat. In any case, his early military service—and perhaps his career— would be a far better experience than that of a conscript from his community.

At the peak of the Cold War, the Soviet officer candidate would likely attend one of 136 military academies scattered throughout the Soviet Union. The Soviet emphasis on military officer training far exceeds any country in the world. In the United States, for example, there are fewer than a dozen full-time military academies. (There are, of course, a number of high school and college ROTC programs in the United States.)

Once commissioned, the Soviet officer accepted an obligation to serve for at least 25 years. Junior officers, not unlike those in the United States, serve their initial tours in their respective specialties. The Soviets also plan for hardship assignments and follow-on professional training. Position and rank stagnation is a natural consequence of the extraordinary number of officers in the Soviet services.

The typical Soviet officer came from a small town or village in Russia or the Ukraine. (The officer candidate route is one way to avoid conscription as well as the rigors of rural farm life.) The candidate must be fluent in native Russian, a requirement that generally excludes ethnic minorities with Asian heritage—some candidates of Asian heritage were chosen for selective assignments, however.

Except for ship, submarine, and strategic rocket force training and duty, the average officer candidate "breezes" through a notably lax training program. Political influence has usually been the ladder to military promotions, and Soviet officers have little prestige among their civilian counterparts. By some estimates, officers rate "4 or less on a scale of 10" among Soviet civilians and businessmen. This low ranking may be mainly due to the officers' general arrogance and a perception that they enjoy both special privileges and higher living standards. Many of these factors date back to a history of military overlords and "ruling class superiority."

Characterizations of Soviet military officers range from "boorish" to "stupid" and "drunks." It is likely that many of these characterizations came from former conscripts who personally witnessed the conduct of their "superiors"—but civilian observations of officers in various states of drunkenness has been the rule rather than the exception. Nor has corruption been unknown among Soviet military officers; many have not been above "working the system" for money or favors. Selling easily acquired vodka and specialty items through the "black market" has been, and likely still is, one of the most prevalent abuses. The selling of awards, decorations, and choice assignments has also been a flourishing "business." It has not been uncommon for a commander to send a young officer or NCO home on leave for an extended period—if he happened to be from an area where choice liqueurs, caviar, or furs could be easily acquired and brought back to his benefactor. Promotions have been easily acquired through this process.

Unit inspections have also been lucrative for both the inspector and the inspected unit's commander. The enterprising commander—of an army combat unit, a bomber or intercontinental ballistic missile command, or a Naval unit—seldom fell below the desired grading standard. The inspector received immediate material rewards and the commander's unit received high ratings on the inspection. Soviet officers, who have readily admitted the prevalence of corruption within the services, defend themselves by pointing out that their corruption is very small in comparison to their civilian counterparts.

Soviet military leaders never openly condoned corruption, of course. When Andropov became secretary general, he lectured the Central Committee on corruption, protection of public property, and abuses of office by public and military officials. Soviet leaders also used the *Red Star* to convey that message, and President Gorbachev issued a plea for integrity and honesty among public officials. Were these public pleas effective? Hardly! Activities involving corruption, black market activities, and *Mafia*-type crimes are reportedly more prevalent than ever. However, some of today's perceived prevalence may be due to increased visibility within an increasingly open society. In any case, Russian military corruption reflects a heritage that is deeply rooted in more than 1,100 years of cultural and social history.

Regarding the "glut" of military officers and the lack of confidence in either enlisted men or NCOs, a story has been told about the cruiser *Sverdlovsk* when it was sent to Britain for Queen Elizabeth's coronation in 1952. There were raves about the conduct and sharpness of the Soviet crew. Later, it was revealed that the 900-man crew consisted entirely of specially selected and heavily drilled officers—there was not a single enlisted man aboard the ship.

Attendance at advanced professional schools for officers was a mandatory requirement for advancement. However, according to some who either attended or taught courses there, the schools did not receive high marks for academic challenges or in-depth training. Edward Lozansky, a former secretary for a human rights commission in the Soviet Union who was later deposed, taught physics at the Military Academy of Armored Forces. According to him, the academic standards at that prestigious advanced course for middle-grade officers were mediocre at best; the physics courses he taught were equivalent to those of a high school course in the United States. Even then, it was a stiff challenge for most of the captains and majors who attended. Their average grades ranged from "C" to "D."

Most of the officers came from small communities, far away from Moscow and Leningrad, and most would spend their careers rotating among military posts far removed from urban areas. Ordinarily, only those with "political pull" were able to get posted closer to cosmopolitan life. There are stories, however, of officers languishing in "backwater" locations, overlooked for attendance at professional schools, who found themselves selected to attend a school because they "did a favor" for an influential senior officer. Such an officer was Lt Col Ivan Dimitrivich Yershov, who was "withering away" at Kushka on the Afghan border when his unhappy wife left him and moved to Moscow. Shortly after arriving there, she casually met a senior general's wife, Galena Sokolov, and they became fast friends. Within months, Yershov was selected to attend the Academy of the General Staff. After graduation, he was assigned to the General Staff in Moscow and promoted to colonel. Within a few years, he was promoted to lieutenant general.

Similar "success stories" have occurred in other military forces, of course, but Yershov's story doesn't end there. He became Chief of Staff of the Kiev Defense Ministry, a position that carried promise for even greater things to come. His daughter Tatyana, over the protests of her parents, married a Jew who was an ardent supporter of Andrei Sakharov. When the KGB reported this situation, Yershov was promptly retired—under circumstances not becoming a Soviet officer. All the "perks" he had enjoyed disappeared. Even his earlier benefactor shunned him.

The man Tatyana Yershov married was Edward Lozansky, who became a vocal militant for human rights. Soon after he began expressing his views openly to staff college students, Lozansky was exiled from the Soviet Union with the promise that his wife could join him later. She was not allowed to leave the Soviet Union, however, until President Jimmy Carter personally intervened seven years later.

Unrest was prevalent throughout the Soviet military. Officers fared better than conscripts, whose plight bordered on forced serfdom, but none were safe from the system's potential wrath. According to many observers, life in the Soviet military was miserable and unpredictable for all. Generals had it best, but even they were not entirely safe. Colonels and below lived a life mostly filled with fear of their superiors. Remember that Stalin, fearful of his senior military officers, purged the Red Army of its senior leadership in 1937. After World War II, he "exiled" Marshal Zhukov, the Soviet's top military leader and popular hero of the war, to the Odessa Military District in the Ukraine. Later appointed Minister of Defense by Khrushchev, Zhukov found himself removed from a prominent post yet again—this time for posing a political threat within the Politburo.

There has been little opportunity for Western military observers to observe or interact with their Soviet counterparts. Gen Nathan Twining, chairman of the Joint Chiefs of Staff, visited the Soviet Union after the war; the next visit by US officials did not take place until 1969. Only occasionally did senior Soviet officers attend official social functions at the US Embassy in Moscow. Only since the late 1980s have émigré reports, firsthand observations, and written materials surfaced regarding the internal activities of Soviet military forces. We have also learned from several Soviet officers who defected. Lt Victor Belenko, a Soviet pilot, flew a MiG 25 out of the

Soviet Union and turned it over to the west. I attended a small-group interview with Belenko in 1976, when he was being "showcased" to a few US military officers by the Intelligence Community. The young Soviet lieutenant told of being stationed near Salsk, deep in Southern Russia. He said the aviators at the base flew very little and drank a lot. He described Salsk, a city of 60,000, as the most drab, dingy, and environmentally poor town he had ever seen. The unpaved streets turned to mud and ruts most of the year. To get inside one of the two movie houses or the few restaurants, one had to wait for hours—then one found that neither the movie nor the food was worth the wait or the money.

Belenko's next assignment was to a Soviet fighter-interceptor base near Chuguyevka, in Eastern Siberia. In Chuguyevka, there was neither a movie theatre, a restaurant, nor any street lights. It was this posting that gave him the encouragement he needed to fly his MiG-25 out to Japan. His revelations about living conditions, moral conduct, and general disorder were very much like others we had seen and heard before.

The Party and Discipline

There were two powerful and influential forces that worked within the Soviet Military Services that would be difficult to imagine in the west. The KGB was strongly intertwined within the Soviet military; its tentacles extended throughout the service branches, and its agents were always on the lookout for evidence of disloyalty and apolitical leanings. They seldom looked for corruption or moral misbehavior unless they were building a case against a targeted individual. The other force always in play was the "Zampolit," the political officer. Lenin originated the political officer concept shortly after the Revolution as a means of monitoring the loyalist remnants of the Tsar's army and as a purveyor of communist doctrine to the masses. The Bolsheviks characterized the Zampolit mission as a "program of public enlightenment."

As the communist movement engulfed Russia and, later, the Soviet Union, the Zampolit concept became an integral part of every military commander's functional responsibility.

Virtually every recruit and officer candidate had already come in contact with a Zampolit during his indoctrination in the Dosaaf or the Komsomol. The Zampolit, an avowed and aggressive communist zealot, was specially trained for his role. The higher the command level he interacted with, the greater his special training to deal with senior officers at the highest level. The Zampolit's early mission was to find and dispel any and all signs of religion or religious overtones expressed by young people, and to "imbue in military personnel the atheistic world-outlook through which they could learn to recognize all that is excellent and noble lies in communist morality."

The Zampolits were in a large sense evangelists of the most ardent communist style. A few of their "attack lines" are included here:

Unauthorized barbaric methods of war-making are characteristic of the U.S. Army. We know for instance of the unseemly role performed by the 'Special Forces' and the 'Green Berets.' Their basic requirements are to have strong fists, a minimum of intellect and a faultless reputation for sadism and cruelty. The mission of these cut-throats also includes appropriate conditioning of other U.S. troops to secure a similar level of expertise in inhuman actions, a propaganda arm with close ties to the 'John Birch Society' and the 'Minutemen,' and in combination they conduct schools on anti-communism and hate seminars.

Chaplains act, not only as reactionary propagandists but also as spies and spiritual overseers, specialists in detecting political nonconformity and unreliability. This may be a classic case of 'the pan calling the kettle black'! Air Force chaplains instill in the pilot's conscience an obscurantist attitude concerning 'the inevitability of wars' and enkindle in them a spirit of bellicosity, self-confidence, and aggressiveness. The large majority of air crew officers are believers that they are 'God's apostles.'

[Air Command bomber crews were] carriers of death and [are] those who are indoctrinated with misanthropic and chauvinistic views and ready on the word of command to drop bombs on peaceful cities of the Soviet Union and other socialist countries.

Many Soviet commanders 'crossed swords' with their assigned Zampolits over issues of decision making, unit supervision, discipline, and so forth. There is strong evidence that the political officer usually won. The cases of General Yershov and Marshall Zhukov carry strong overtones of KGB and Zampolit influence.

145

The Soviet Triad

The Soviet strategic forces were similar to those of the United States, with the Soviets placing a greater emphasis on ICBMs and SSBN/SLBMs than on strategic bombers. The Strategic Rocket Force (SRF), the fifth major branch of the Soviet Armed Forces, was first identified in 1960. It immediately became the preeminent service and was given the highest priority for selection of recruits and officer candidates. The military commissariats, the Komsomols, and the Dosaafs were alerted to be on the lookout for exceptionally talented and bright students to be conscripted for the SRF. The sole mission of the SRF was to operate the ICBM force. Second in priority was the Long-Range Air Force (LRA). Candidates for both the SRF and the LRA usually came from the "educationally privileged" sector of Soviet society. The LRA enjoyed a more attractive "calling card" for young officer candidates, but the SRF had priority. Political "string-pulling" played a large role in determining which branch would get the candidate.

The LRA candidate would probably have completed up to 300 hours of flying training in a precadet program before he attended the academy. SRF and LRA candidates attended four-year academy programs that included most of the basic university courses. Perhaps the major difference between a Soviet military academy and a US military academy is that a Zampolit is always present in the Soviet academy, ensuring that the required courses in Marxist-Leninist history and economics—the history of the Communist Party—are adequately provided and attended. The LRA student will receive an additional 240 hours of flying training concurrently with his academic schedule.

At the conclusion of the academy course, the new officer is commissioned as a lieutenant; in the LRA, the new lieutenant is also commissioned as a Pilot Engineer Third Class. The most unusual feature of the LRA is that officers, sometimes up to the grade of major, are assigned as aircraft crew chiefs. These assignments are made because the LRA does not have sufficient numbers of qualified NCOs and because putting officers in crew chief positions establishes responsibility in the position. The Soviets attempted to install the rank of ensign or warrant officer to bridge the gap between the enlisted grades, but the program was defeated because junior officers usually "adopted" the ensigns as menservants rather than fitting them in the chain of command. The ensigns also were given officer privileges, which further removed them from their intended use.

Russia and the Soviet Union have had a sea service throughout their history, and it remains an honorable service. The Soviet Navy's SSBN operations suffered along with the other services in procuring quality recruits to serve aboard the highly technical nuclear submarines. The Soviet Navy normally consists of 20 percent officers, 10 percent warrant officers, and 70 percent conscripts. The officers and warrant officers have lengthy service commitments, but the Navy receives the lowest priority in recruit selection. The "brawn over brain" syndrome for Russian sailors dates back to the old sailing days. There has been evidence, however, that emphasis has shifted in recent years toward high-quality enlisted technicians for SSBN operations. Nevertheless, the manning ratio of officers to enlisted men on Russian SSBN submarines remains far greater than that of SSBNs in the US Navy and other Western navies. Although a firm ratio cannot be determined for today's Russian SSBNs, the *Sverdlovsk* story indicates that the Soviet Navy had real manning problems in its SSBN force.

It also appears that the navy suffered the greatest personnel turnover of all Soviet services—an estimated 70 percent every three years, with one-sixth of those leaving every six months. One can only guess at the Soviet Navy's training load and the concern for proficiency and war-fighting ability that may exist among its leaders. Consistent documentation has reflected that the Soviet sailor lived "under conditions not seen in Western navies in over fifty years," with miserable pay, unusually harsh discipline at sea, and the traditional over-abundance of communist indoctrination.

Finally, I think it is interesting to review the military personnel force structure of the Soviet Union during the Cold War, placing it in perspective with what "we thought we knew" versus what "they wanted us to know." At the peak of the Cold War, the United States had approximately 2.2 million men and women in its military services; the Soviets maintained approximately 5.8 million men and women in its five service branches. While the percentage of women in the Soviet military cannot be determined, the total numbers reflect a ratio of more than 2½ to 1 in favor of the Soviets. Evidence from various sources suggests that the 5.8 million men and women in Soviet military service were assigned as indicated below.

(1) 650,000 were assigned to internal security and border guard duty, many along innocuous country borders and shorelines; most would have been irrelevant if hostilities had broken out.

(2) 100,000 were assigned to civil defense duties, preparing and maintaining underground nuclear shelters.

(3) 920,000 in uniform (mostly conscripts who had low academic standings, were politically unreliable, or were generally regarded as unfit for combat duty) were assigned to public road and railroad construction and maintenance, many across the Trans-Siberian plane.

(4) 560,000 manned the extraordinary network of aircraft and missile defense systems extended across the Soviet Union. (The US average was about 8,000 to operate its air defense systems.)

(5) 70,000 troops were assigned to the occupation force in Czechoslovakia.

(6) 30,000 were assigned to the occupation force in Poland.

(7) The number of Soviet troops "maintaining the balance" in East Germany was obscured; estimates range from 30,000 to 100,000.

(8) 495,000 Soviet troops were maintained along the Chinese border.

(9) Approximately 472,000 were assigned to the Soviet strategic forces: bombers, ICBMs, SSBNs. (US Strategic Air Command and Navy SSBN crews numbered fewer than 100,000.)

(10) More than 100,000 Soviet troops were assigned to Soviet military airlift forces. (US Military Airlift Command averaged approximately 37,000 personnel.)

(11) Approximately 250,000 were assigned to the Soviet Defense Ministry in Moscow and the other major Soviet headquarters. (US forces in the Pentagon averaged 60,000.)

(12) 10,000 Soviet troops were assigned to coastal defense artillery units.

(13) Thousands of troops are assigned to parade duty at Alabino, just outside Moscow.

(14) More than 70,000 Soviets were assigned as Zampolit political officers. (Some 3,300 chaplains are assigned to all US services.)

By coincidence, I was in Kiev, Ukraine, in the Summer of 1992. Riding through downtown Kiev, I commented to my Ukrainian host that there appeared to be quite a number of Soviet military officers walking along the streets. He replied, "Too many!" I looked to the interpreter sitting behind us and asked, "Where are they all going?" She responded without hesitation, "They aren't going anywhere! They have no place to go. I see the same colonels every day walk along this street with their 'prestigious' flat briefcases, with nothing in them. Then they walk down the other side, all day long, trying to look important." I asked whether they were Ukrainian officers or Russian. She said, "Russian; there are many Ukrainians in the Soviet Army, but most of them are far away." Only on few occasions did I see enlisted men—and then in a military bus or open-bed truck, or grouped together in a train car—never singularly on the street. They always appeared to be kept away from the public.

The foregoing assessment constitutes a critical analysis of the Soviet Armed Forces and a serious indictment of their war-fighting capability during the Cold War. One only has to extrapolate the revealed character, morale, and social decay among its military forces to wonder how efficient and capable they might have been. Military power, as represented by vast numbers of troops in uniform, was always important to the Soviets. Using similar reasoning, they placed equal emphasis on massive numbers of weapon systems.

These large numbers were implanted in the minds of the west by Soviet propaganda, extravagant May Day demonstrations of capability, and, to a large extent, by our own media. But the true picture seems to suggest that the *perceived* one was created with "smoke and mirrors." The United States and its allies relied heavily on perceptions of Soviet power from the outset of the Cold War. It was these perceptions that greatly promoted development of the largest weapons programs ever known—on both sides of the Iron Curtain. Most would argue, however, that we had little choice since Soviet "smoke" obscured accurate assessments and the "mirror" reflected both ways.

Epilogue

The world has become in many respects a much safer place than during the Cold War. Unfortunately, it is also still a dangerous place, fraught with uncertainty.

—Gen Eugene E. Habiger
Commander in Chief
United States Strategic Command
Statement before the
Senate Armed Services Committee
13 March 1997

The (Russian) missile force is in the same state of readiness as ten years ago. My men and missiles are always ready.

—Gen of the Army Igor Sergeyev
Minister of Defense,
Republic of Russia
Interview,
  Novosti Daily Review Moscow
19 June 1997

The Cold War has ended. No formal surrender, no capitulation, no declaration by either party that the protracted impasse is over. Most traditional historians would say that wars don't end this way; but from mid-twentieth century, this has been the pattern of concluding hostilities by the United States and its allies. Korea, the first hostile engagement after World War II, ended in an unresolved truce; two decades later, a similar "truce" concluded a ten-year impasse in Vietnam. Other engagements that have ended in neutrality include the Soviet thrusts at Berlin and Cuba, and the cease-fire at the conclusion of Desert Storm. The ending of the Cold War was consistent with these dubious settlements.

The unfortunate circumstance of these impolitic trends is that in each case, the embers continue to glow within the unsettled coals of the fires that once blazed—perhaps lying dormant until an ill wind stirs the flames anew.

The Cold War was singularly unique in the history of US military-political conflicts. It was the longest *standoff* in modern history. The period saw the largest accumulation of the most sophisticated—and the deadliest—weapons ever developed. Fortunately, none of those weapons of mass destruction were ever used.

The "superpowers" engaged in *roller coaster* diplomacy through numerous changes in political persuasion within both governments as the old leaders in the Soviet Union died and political "solutions" seesawed back and forth in the United States. The period of conflict witnessed numerous deadly "sub-wars" fought both directly and indirectly between the two major adversaries *under the umbrella* of the Cold War. And the span of time saw sons and daughters of earlier Cold Warriors on both sides replacing their fathers in the bombers, tankers, submarines, and missile silos.

Beneath that *umbrella*, the Soviet Union used virtually every means it could muster to promote the communist manifesto. The Soviets exited World War II with more technology and economic stability than had existed at any previous time in their turbulent history. Having taken full advantage of Western lend-lease programs, and having stolen industries, technologies, and skilled German engineers and scientists, Stalin installed himself as a national hero. Robust with power and ego, Stalin made an early postwar declaration that war with capitalistic governments was inevitable as long as those governments existed.

The Democratic People's Republic of Korea became a Soviet satellite in large part because US forces were stretched too thin to prevent Soviet domination of the North Koreans during the closing days of the war with Japan. Stalin moved swiftly as the war came to a close, mopping up Japanese occupiers with little resistance from either a weakened Japan or the Allies. On the Western Front, he attempted to exert absolute control over Berlin. Failing in that effort, he looked for other opportunities to test US vulnerability.

Stalin found his opportunity in Korea. North Korean troops, fully armed and trained by the Red Army, moved swiftly across the 38th parallel into South Korea on 25 June 1950. The North Koreans were soon backed by several hundred thousand Chinese Army troops who had positioned them-selves to ambush the United Nations forces when they pushed the North Koreans back into their own territory. The Korean

War had a dramatic impact on the Cold War and on US policy. It created an economic and military drain on the United States, and it presented the challenge of fighting on the other side of the world as Soviet military strength was building in Europe. And, although atomic weapons were deployed with SAC bombers, US policy was to employ them only as a last resort.

Containment of communism remained the US policy objective. The Korean War became a disaster in every way—politically, economically, and militarily, causing a tragic loss of war fighters' lives. An estimated 54,000 American fighting men were killed in action and 300,000 were wounded. Paradoxically, the Soviet Union, which had orchestrated the invasion to foster its own objectives, recorded no official casualties. SAC's B-29 bombers and RB-29 reconnaissance aircraft participated heavily in the war.

SAC operations accounted for 21,328 sorties, including almost 2,000 "recce" missions. Sixteen B-29s were lost to Soviet-built MiGs, four to antiaircraft fire. B-29 gunners accounted for 33 enemy aircraft kills, including 16 MiGs. When the cease-fire truce was finally negotiated, SAC combat crews returned to their "regular" Cold War mission responsibilities.

A scant twelve years later, in 1965, the United States once again found itself falling victim to another communist incursion, this time in Vietnam. And SAC combat crews were again taken from their nuclear deterrence mission and sent to fight a conventional war. This time, bomber, tanker, and reconnaissance crews retrained in a variety of fighter and support aircraft to support the effort. In the latter years of the ten-year conflict, B-52s, including the later B-52G model, were reconfigured to deliver conventional bombs. Sent to operate out of Guam and Thailand, they were heavily employed in the war effort. The United States saw five presidents preside over the worst political, military, and image-defeating debacle in our history.

"How did the United States get into the war and why did it stay so long?" "How could a nation with the technology and superior might to destroy the world permit itself to be fought to a virtual draw by a small and untrained *ragtag* army of peasants?" These questions may never be satisfactorily answered, but Americans fought and died in Vietnam. That is what they were asked to do and that is what they did. The

Cold Warriors who manned the B-52s flew over 126,000 sorties during the conflict; the recce and tanker crews flew untold thousands of missions. Air Force EB-66s, along with Navy EA-3s and EA-6s, provided electronic jamming. F-105s, F-4s, F-111s, and A-7s flew suppression missions to keep Soviet-provided MiGs on the ground and SAM sites down.

In the end, Americans watched North Vietnamese tanks and troops march into Saigon as US Embassy personnel and their Marine guards scrambled to evacuate. During both Korea and Vietnam, two tragic tests of will, American fighting men and women "stood tall"; they never wavered from their call to duty. The Soviet Union once again "laid low," obviously waiting for the United States to buckle or bankrupt itself—*but it didn't!* The importance of these events and circumstances lies in their reflection of a great nation's strength, commitment, and resolve—*but at no small cost!* It is also important to note that, while both of these conflicts severely stretched US strategic nuclear deterrence forces, SAC maintained *40 percent* of its B-52Gs and Hs, and *100 percent* of its ICBMs, on full alert. At the same time, Navy's SSBN force maintained coverage of all essential Soviet targets. These were costly periods in terms of lost lives and lost resources, both physical and economical; but US strategic deterrence remained effective: *The Soviets stood fast!*

From the perspective of both the people and the fighting forces of the United States, the Soviet Union held a loaded gun at the head of the west throughout the Cold War and was prepared to pull the trigger at any moment of perceived US weakness. The Soviet Cold Warrior was touted as "ten feet tall and made of steel." These were the underlying *perceptions* of the west. In developing this manuscript, I reviewed more than 30 speeches I made during my senior officer years and found a consistent theme—that the Soviet military force was massive and strong, and was technologically capable of destroying the United States and its allies. This was the general theme of most Cold War talks and lectures because it was what we believed, based on the information available. Consequently, the words of Western leaders and experts were translated into requirements for offensive and defensive military systems to counter any attack by highly capable and elite Soviet forces.

US intelligence reports, almost always backed by photographic, electronic, and/or human evidence, steadily fed and kindled the flames of Soviet military capabilities.

That this perception was somewhat overstated is by no means the fault of US information-gathering systems and organizations. The Iron Curtain provided a near-absolute shroud around Soviet political and military regimes—and the Soviets skillfully practiced the crafts of misinformation, disinformation, propaganda, and *mackorova* (masquerade). Capabilities were often "manufactured" to keep the west speculating and to create false impressions for internal consumption by the Soviet people. No other government in history ever held such a sustained totalitarian grip or such an ironclad ideology as did the Soviet Union—neither Hitler nor Mao created, executed, or sustained anything close to the virtually absolute control exerted by Stalin and his successors.

In 1981, after previous administrations had "experimented and toyed" for decades with strategies to bring the Cold War to a close, President Ronald Reagan introduced a straightforward and simple dictum: *Prevent war by maintaining military capabilities sufficient to win a potential war and demonstrate the unyielding determination to use whatever it takes to do so*—and to remain consistent, thereby persuading any adversary that the costs of attacking the United States would exceed any possible benefits. The Reagan strategy was described as requiring effectiveness based upon four premises.

Survivability: The ability of US forces to survive a preemptive nuclear attack with sufficient resilience and retaliatory strength to inflict losses on the perpetrator that would outweigh his potential gain.

Credibility: US capability to respond to an attack must be of a sufficient amount that any potential aggressor would believe that the nation *could* and *would* use it.

Clarity: Actions of any potential aggressor that are *not* acceptable must be sufficiently clear to all potential aggressors so they know what they must not do.

Safety: The potential for failure of any nuclear system through accident, unauthorized use, or miscalculation must be minimized.

With these precepts in mind, President Reagan boldly announced a dramatic expansion of capabilities to support the strategy:

B-1 Bomber: The previously canceled bomber would be built and deployed. *Missiles:* Ground-launched cruise missiles (GCM) and *Pershing II*s would be deployed with US forces assigned to NATO.

Strategic Defense Initiative: The theoretical notion of a Strategic Defense Initiative (SDI) program was publicly announced.

The SDI (Star Wars) initiative was far more alarming and provocative to the Soviets than any other threat posed by the United States during the Cold War. Reagan's initiatives, although exceptionally costly, brought on dramatic *winds of change* in the attitudes of Soviet leaders. They also prompted the beginning of an unprecedented economic growth in the United States—a growth that persists today, with rapid developments in technology and a restoration of public confidence. Perhaps most important, these initiatives projected a perception of US strength and will to the leaders of the Soviet Union.

We cannot diminish the importance of Mikhail Gorbachev's arrival on the Soviet political stage during this dramatic period of demonstrated determination by the US president. Gorbachev no doubt hastened the process of disintegration within the Soviet Union (as compared to what might have been under his predecessor); nevertheless, Reagan's initiatives were the beginning of the end.

As the Iron Curtain began to fall away, eventually gaping full open, the unabridged spectacle of the Soviet Union's skeletal framework was laid bare. The revelations took the West by shocking surprise. No one could have remotely imagined or speculated how frail and devastated the whole of the communist empire was, or how long it had been in a state of despair. It was the dire conditions of the people that shocked most.

Analysts will work for years to estimate the real depth and substance of Soviet war-fighting capabilities—despite Sergeyev's quoted assessment, above. There was little question regarding the Soviets' conventional land warfare capabilities, mainly due to the massive numbers of soldiers in uniform. The question regarding the *will* of those men to fight cannot be answered, although history has witnessed consistent losses by Russian armies engaged in wars, including World War II until they were substantially fortified by the Western Allies. There is considerable evidence that the Soviets had developed land- and sea-based ballistic missiles as well as strategic bombers near equal to those of the United States. But there are questions regarding the efficiency and reliability of those systems and the will of Soviet military forces to use them. It is now reasonably apparent that the United States and its allies were virtually held hostage as much by *smoke and mirrors* and an almost leak-proof society as by real substance.

These are my impressions, and those of many others, of the surprise and shock of Westerners upon seeing the disorder and desolation of a vast nation, its cities and its people, when the cloak of secrecy eventually opened. After my successive visits over a five-year period to the Soviet Union and then the former Soviet states, I understood the full and devastating effects of a communist social order. The old jokes about Soviet inefficiency, comical failures, and a lackadaisical people enduring personal misery while coping with bureaucratic bungling—all suddenly became too real; they were not jokes at all, and they were definitely not funny.

Meanwhile, I could not forget my almost 40 years of being convinced that this was a *superpower* of the highest and most efficient order—one that had created an elite war-fighting force second to none. As I surveyed the scenes before me during my many stays in Moscow, Leningrad (St. Petersburg), Kiev, and Minsk, I frequently reflected on the gleaming cities and homes back in the States—great interstate highways, giant sky-scrapers, comfortable homes with groomed landscapes, and a well-fed, well-dressed populace that was generally satisfied. In the former Soviet Union, I mostly saw vast potholes in the streets of Moscow, and horse-drawn carts moving along with the traffic in all of the major cities. I saw rotting produce and cheap goods, dingy and run-down buildings, and filth everywhere. But most of all, I saw throngs of pitiful people wandering the streets on the lookout for anything opportune. Except for the lack of war-torn physical damage and battle casualties, Russia and the former Soviet Union states reflected the consequences of war. The government and the military infrastructure have fallen into disarray, the economy is in virtual collapse, millions of displaced people wander the streets, and poverty is at an all-time high. At no other time in recorded history have events unfolded in such a bizarre manner as did the failure of Soviet communism and the end of the Cold War.

Nor has any other time seen so much so freely given to recover adversarial nations as that given to the former communist republics. And yet, as has been witnessed and continues to be, no previous recovering nation has so frivolously squandered the relief given as have these former communist republics. They have freely permitted relief aid to fall into the hands of their former political and military bureaucrats. It is also apparent that even though the United States and its Western allies won the Cold War theoretically, the spoils did not necessarily go to the victors. When I was a Cold Warrior, I perceived the Soviet Union as a superpower. When I traveled to Russia and other states after the Cold War had ended, my earlier impressions quickly faded. And it was the menacing *Soviet Bear* that, despite its having "baited" the West in Berlin, Korea, Cuba, Vietnam, and dozens of other lesser-known areas, bankrupted its economy and its people in pursuit of a fraudulent social order.

Today, the shadows of the Cold Warriors who stood the test remain vividly long and indelible, reminding us that they fought in a quiet war of nerves through four and one-half decades. They served through a revolution of weapon systems technologies more dramatic than in any previous period in history. But the revolutionary growth in those technologies and operational hardware, while extraordinary, did not compare with the dedication of the people who *chose* to walk a different path. "*Chose*" is important because the men and women who sustained the entire US strategic nuclear deterrent force chose to serve their country. To their ever-lasting credit, they chose patriotism and service to country over other available pursuits. Not a single draftee or conscript served aboard a SAC aircraft, in an ICBM launch control center, or aboard a nuclear submarine. The Cold Warriors rode through a tide of soaring technology achievements, erratic changes in perceptions of military prestige, and radical social changes. Yet, they continued to come forward—and when they moved on, others with the same ideals followed. The term *professional* seems not quite enough to embody or characterize the Cold Warrior, but I cannot think of another term that better describes those who willingly served, sacrificed, and excelled during one of the greatest periods of threat our country has ever known.

I have attempted herein to honor the Cold Warriors, to accurately characterize their responsibilities and challenges, and to reminisce about their great war-fighting machines. I have recalled some "war stories," smiled a bit at the fun and the not-so-fun times, paid tribute to those who made the supreme sacrifice, and recognized the spouses and families who "came along for the ride and kept the home fires warm."

I have also reviewed perhaps the saddest spectacles of the Cold War—the *reluctant warriors* of the Soviet Union and the plight of their homeland during the unwarranted siege imposed by their own leaders. While the major opponents sparred during the almost 50 years of the "odd war," the only direct shots fired were at US surveillance aircraft, or those *"mistakenly thought to be so,"* over or near Soviet territory. But it may also be said that the world had almost 50 years of global peace—peace, however, that was neither tranquil nor assured at any given time.

So the Cold War has ended! *Or has it?* As we knew it, yes; but the world today perhaps remains *just* as unstable as it was during the 45-year stalemate. 'Lest we heed the words of the two former Cold Warriors at the beginning of this final passage.

Bibliography

Books

Adams, James T. *The March of Democracy: America and World Power.* vol. 4. New York: Charles Scribner's Sons, 1940.

Aganbeggan, Abel G. *Perestroika Annual.* Vol. 2. Washington, D.C.: Brassey's (US), Inc., 1989.

Agee, Joseph L., and Robert H. *Soviet Foreign Policy since World War II.* New York: Pergamon Press, 1988.

Aiken, Jonathan. *Nixon—A Life.* New York: Regency Publishing, Inc.,1993.

Anderson, David A. *Strategic Air Command: Two-Thirds of the Triad.* New York: Scribner's, 1976.

Anderson, William R. *Atomic Submarines.* Chicago: Children's Press, 1961.

Arbotov, Georgi. The System. New York: Random House, 1992.

———. *The Soviet Viewpoint.* New York: Dodd, Mead & Co., 1983.

Area Handbook for the Soviet Union. Washington, D.C.: The American University, 1971.

Armstrong, John. *Ideology, Politics, and Government in the Soviet Union.* New York: Praeger Publishers, 1970.

Arnold, Anthony. *Afghanistan: The Soviet Invasion in Perspective.* Stanford, Calif.: Hoover Institution Press, 1981.

Aspin Report. *The Strategic Defense Initiative and American Security.* Boston: University Press of America, 1987.

Baar, James, and William E. Howard. *Spacecraft and Missiles of the World.* New York: Harcourt, Brace & World, 1966.

Baldwin, Hanson W. *The Great Arms Race: A Comparison of United States and Soviet Power.* New York: Frederick A. Praeger, 1958.

Ball, Desmond. *Politics and Force Levels: Strategic Missile Program of the Kennedy Administration.* Berkeley, Calif.: University of California Press, 1980.

Barnet, Richard J. *Developing the ICBM: A Study in Bureaucratic Politics.* New York: Columbia University Press: 1976.

———. *The Giants.* New York: Simon & Schuster, 1977.

————. *The Rocket's Red Glare.* New York: Simon & Schuster, 1990.

Bender, David L. *The Cold War: Opposing Viewpoints.* San Diego: Greenhaven Press, Inc., 1992.

Bentley, John. *The Thresher Disaster.* New York: Doubleday & Co., Inc., 1975.

Beschloss, Michael R., *May Day—Eisenhower, Khruschev and the U-2 Affair.* New York: Harper & Row, 1986.

Beschloss, Michael R., and Strobe Talbott. *At the Highest Levels.* Boston: Little, Brown & Co., 1993.

Betts, Richard K. *Soldiers, Statesmen, and Cold War Crisis.* Cambridge, Mass.: Harvard University Press, 1977.

Bialer, Seweryn. *Stalin's Successors.* New York: Cambridge University Press, 1980.

————. *The Soviet Paradox.* New York: Alfred E. Knopf, 1986.

Bittman, Ladislav. *The New Image-Makers: Soviet Propaganda & Disinformation Today.* Washington, D.C.: Pergamon-Brassey's, 1988.

Bohn, John. *Development of Strategic Air Command.* Offutt Air Force Base, Nebr.: Office of the Historian, Headquarters, SAC, 1976.

Bookbinder, Alan, Olivia Lichtenstein, and Richard Denton. *Comrades, Portraits of Soviet Life.* New York: Plume Books, 1986.

Borklund, C.W. *Men of the Pentagon: From Forrestal to McNamara.* New York: Praeger Press, 1966.

Bottome, Edgar M. *The Missile Gap: A Study of The Formulation of Military and Political Policy.* Rutherford, New York: Farleigh Dickinson University Press, 1971.

————. *The Balance of Terror: A Guide to the Arms Race.* Boston: Beacon Press, 1971.

Boyne, Walter. *Boeing B-52, A Documentary History.* New York: Jane's Publishing Co., 1982.

Briggs, B. Bruce. *The Shield of Faith.* New York: Simon & Schuster, Inc., 1988.

Burgess, Eric. *Long-Range Ballistic Missiles.* New York: MacMillan & Co.,1962.

Burton, James G. *The Pentagon Wars.* Annapolis, Md.: Naval Institute Press, 1993.

Carmichael, Joel. *A History of Russia.* New York: Hippocrene Books, 1990.

Carpozi, George, Jr. *Red Spies in Washington.* New York: Simon & Schuster, Inc., 1968.

Carrere, d'Encausse Helene. *Decline of an Empire: The Soviet Socialist Republics in Revolt.* New York: Newsweek Books, 1982.

Chapman, John L. *Atlas, The Story of a Missile.* New York: Harper & Row, 1960.

Chung, Henry. *The Russians Came to Korea.* Seoul, Korea: The Korean Pacific Press, 1947.

Churka, Joseph. *Soviet Breakout.* Washington, D.C.: Pergamon-Brassey's International Defense Publishers, 1988.

Clancy, Tom. *Submarine.* New York: Berkeley Books, 1993.

Clausewitz, Carl von. *On War.* Edited and translated by Michael Howard and Peter Paret. Princeton, New Jersey: Princeton University Press, 1984.

Cockburn, Andrew. *The Threat: Inside the Soviet Military Machine.* New York: Random House, 1983.

Coffee, Thomas M. *Iron Eagle.* New York: Crown Publishers, 1986.

Cohen, Stephen F. *Rethinking the Soviet Experience.* London: Oxford University Press, 1990.

Cox, Arthur M. *The Dynamics of Détente: How To End The Arms Race.* New York: W.W. Norton, 1976.

Current, Richard N., Harry T. Williams, and Frank Freidel. *American History—A Survey.* New York: Alfred A. Knopf, 1965.

Danchenko, A.M. *Military Pedagogy.* Moscow: 1973. (Translated by the US Air Force).

Dicerto, J.J. *Missile Base Beneath the Sea.* New York: St. Martin's Press, 1967.

Divine, Robert. *Eisenhower and the Cold War.* New York: Oxford University Press, 1981.

Dolgikh and Kuraniov. *Communist Ideals and the Atheistic Indoctrination of the Troops.* Moscow: Military Publishing House, 1976.

Donald, David. *Spylane.* Osceola, Wisc.: Motorbooks International, 1987.

Donaldson, Robert H. *The Soviet Union in the Third World: Successes and Failures.* Boulder, Colo.: Westview Press, 1981.

Donovan, Robert J. *Nemesis—Truman and Johnson in the Coils of War in Asia.* St. Martin's-Marek, 1984.

Duignan, Peter, and Rabushka Duignan. *The United States in the 1980s.* Hoover Institution: Stanford University Press, 1980.

Efron, Edith. *The News Twisters.* Los Angeles: Nash Publishing, 1971.

Eisenhower, Dwight D. *Mandate for Change, 1953–1956.* Garden City, N.Y.: Doubleday, 1963.

Elliott, Osborn. *The World of Oz, An Inside Report on Big-Time Journalism.* New York: Viking Press,1980.

Emyehko, A. N. *Kiev: Memory of the Hero City.* Kiev, Ukraine: publisher unknown, 1990.

Feldbaum, Carl B. and Ronald J. Feldbaum. *Looking the Tiger in the Eye.* New York: Harper & Row, 1988.

Gaddis, John Lewis. *Strategies of Containment.* New York: Oxford University Press, 1982.

———. *Russia, the Soviet Union and the United States: An Interpretive History.* New York: John Wiley and Sons, 1978.

Garthoff, Raymond L. *Soviet Military Policy: An Historical Analysis.* New York: Praeger, 1966.

———. *Détente and Confrontation: American-Soviet Relations from Nixon to Reagan.* Washington, D.C.: Brookings Institution, 1985.

Gates, Robert M. *From the Shadows.* New York: Simon & Schuster, 1996.

Ginsberg, Col Robert N. USAF, *U.S. Military Strategy in the Sixties.* New York: W. W. Norton, 1965.

Glynn, Patrick. *Closing Pandora's Box.* New York: Harper Collins, 1992.

Goldhamer, H. *The Soviet Soldier.* New York: Crane Russack, 1975.

Goldman, Eric F. *The Tragedy of Lyndon Johnson.* New York: Dell Books, 1969.

Goldman, Marshall. *Gorbachev's Challenge: Economic Reform in the Age of High Technology.* New York: W. W. Norton, 1987.

Goodchild, Peter. *J. Robert Oppenheimer.* New York: Fromm International 1985.

Gorbachev, Mikhail. *Perestroika.* New York: Harper & Row, 1987.

Gray, Colin S. *The Soviet-American Arms Race.* Farnsborough, U.K.: Saxon Books: 1976.

Grechko, A. A. *The Armed Forces of the Soviet State.* Moscow: Military Publishing House, 1975.

Greider, William. *Who Will Tell the People.* New York: Simon & Schuster, 1992.

Griffin, William E. *The Superpowers and Regional Tensions.* Lexington, Mass.: Lexington Books, 1982.

Griffith, Thomas. *How True: A Skeptic's Guide to Believing the News.* Boston: An Atlantic Monthly Press Book, 1974.

Griffith, William E. *The Soviet Empire: Expansion and Detente.* Lexington, Mass.: Lexington Books, 1976.

Gunston, Bill. *Modern Bombers.* New York: Salamander Books Ltd.,1988.

Halberstadt, Hans. *FB-111 AARDVARK.* Stillwater, Minn.: Specialty Press, 1992.

Harris, Edgar S. Jr., Lt Gen, USAF, Retired. *US Air Force Oral History.* Interview by Lt Col David L. Young, USAF, edited by Pauline Tibbs. Washington, D.C.: Office of Air Force History, 1985.

Herring, George C. *Aid to Russia, 1941–1946: Strategic Diplomacy, the Origins of the Cold War.* New York: Columbia University Press, 1973.

Hersh, Seymour M. *The Target is Destroyed.* New York: Random House, 1986.

Higham, Robin, and Jacob W. Kipp. *Soviet Aviation and Air Power: A Historical View.* Boulder, Colo.: Westview Press, 1977.

Hochman, Stanley, and Eleanor Hochman. *A Dictionary of Contemporary American History.* New York: Signet Books, 1993.

Hollander, Paul. *Soviet and American Society: A Comparison.* New York: Oxford University Press, 1973.

Horelick, Arnold, and Myron Rush. *Strategic Power and Soviet Foreign Policy.* Chicago: University of Chicago Press, 1966.

Hosbawm, Eric. *The Age of Extremes*. New York: Pantheon Books, 1994.

Hosking, Geoffrey. *The Awakening of the Soviet Union*. Cambridge, Mass.: Harvard University Press, 1991.

Hubler, Richard G. *SAC: The Strategic Air Command*. New York: Duell, Sloan & Pearce, 1958.

Hughes, Gweneth, and Simon Welfare. *Red Empire*. London: Weidenfeld & Nicholson, 1990.

Huntington, Samuel P. *The Common Defense*. New York: Columbia University Press, 1961.

Hyland, William G. *The Reagan Foreign Policy*. New York: New American Library, 1987.

Ilinskiy, I. *What is the Komsomol?* Moscow: Novosti Publishers, 1978.

Infield, Glenn B. *Unarmed and Unafraid*. London: MacMillan & Co., 1970.

Inkeles, A. *Public Opinion in Soviet Russia*. Boston: Harvard University Press, 1950.

Jane's All The World's Greatest Aircraft. London: Jane's Publishing, Ltd., 1979–80.

Jacobsen, Meyers K., and Ray Wagner. *B-36 in Action*. Carrollton, Texas, Signal Publications, 1980.

Jordon, Amos A., and William J. Taylor. *American National Security: Policy and Process*. Baltimore: Johns Hopkins University Press, 1981.

Kahn, Herman. *Thinking about the Unthinkable in the 1980s*. New York: Simon & Schuster, 1984.

Kahan, Jerome H. *Security in the Nuclear Age: Developing US Strategic Arms Policy*. Washington, D.C.: Brookings Institution, 1975.

Kalb, Marvin, and Bernard Kalb. *Kissinger*. New York: Dell Books, 1975.

Kanter, MacKinley. *Mission with LeMay: My Story*. Garden City, N.Y.: Doubleday, 1965.

Kassoff, A. *The Soviet Youth Programme*. Boston: Harvard University Press: 1965.

Katz, Nick. *Wild Blue Yonder: Politics and the B-1 Bomber*. New York: Pantheon Books, 1988.

Kaufman, William W. *The McNamara Strategy*. New York: Harper & Row: 1964.

Kearns, Doris. *Lyndon Johnson and the American Dream*. New York: Harper & Row, 1976.

Keep, John L. H. *Soldiering in Tsarist Russia*. Washington, D.C.: The Harmon Memorial Lectures, Office of Air Force History, 1988.

Kennan, George F. *The Nuclear Delusion*. New York: Pantheon Books, 1982.

————. *The Cloud of Danger: Current Realities of American Foreign Policy*. Boston: Little, Brown & Co., 1977.

Kennedy, Robert F. *Thirteen Days*. New York: W.W. Norton & Co., 1969.

Khrushchev, Nikita. *Khruschev Remembers: The Last Testament*. Edited and translated by Strobe Talbott. Boston: Little, Brown & Co., 1974.

————. *Necessity for Choice*. New York: Harper & Row, 1961.

Kissinger, Henry. *Diplomacy*. New York: Simon & Schuster, 1994.

Knorr, Klaus. *Historical Dimensions of National Security Problems*. Lawrence, Kans.: University Press of Kansas, 1976.

Koenig, William, and Peter Scofield. *Soviet Military Power*. New York: Gallery Books, 1983.

Kohn, Richard, and Joseph P. Harahan. *Strategic Warfare*. Washington, D.C.: Office of Air Force History, 1988.

Kolkowicz, R. *The Soviet Military and the Communist Party*. Princeton, N. J.: Princeton University Press, 1967.

Kostikov, N.A. *A Complete Approach to the Training of Pre-Call up Youth*. Moscow: DOSAAF Publishers, 1980.

Kozlov, S.N. *The Officer's Handbook*. Moscow: Military Publishing House, 1971.

Kuniholm, Bruce R. *The Origins of the Cold War in the Near East*. Princeton, N. J.: Princeton University Press, 1980.

Laird, Melvin R. *A House Divided: America's Strategy Gap*. Chicago: Henry Regnery, 1962.

Laqueur, Walter. *Stalin*. New York: Scribner's, 1990.

Leckie, Robert. *The Wars of America—vol. 2, San Juan Hill to Tonkin*. New York: Harper & Row, 1968.

Lee, Asher. *The Soviet Air Force.* New York: John Day, 1962.

Lewin, Moshe. *The Gorbachev Phenomenon.* Berkeley, Calif.: University of California Press, 1991.

Lippman, Walter. *The Cold War: A Study in US Foreign Policy.* New York: Harper, 1947.

Love, Jay, and Neal Kimmel. *Peacemaker: The History of the B-36 at Carswell AFB, 1948–1958.* Fort Worth, Tex.: Fort Worth Taylor Publishing Co., 1995.

Luttwak, Edward N. *The Grand Strategy of the Soviet Union.* New York: St. Martin's Press, 1983.

Marbut, F. B. *News from the Capital: The Story of Washington Reporting.* Carbondale, Ill.: Southern Illinois University Press, 1971.

Mastny, Vojtech. *Russia's Road to the Cold War: Diplomacy, Warfare and the Politics of Communism.* New York: Columbia University Press, 1979.

Mayer, Martin. *Making News.* Garden City, N.Y.: Doubleday & Co., Inc., 1987.

McDonald, Callum A. *Korea, The War Before Vietnam.* New York: Free Press, A Divison of Macmillan, Inc., 1986.

McNamara, Robert S. *The Essence of Security.* New York: Harper & Row, 1968.

Menzel, Paul. *Moral Arguments and the War in Vietnam.* Nashville, Tenn.: Aurora Publishers, Inc., 1971.

Mickiewicz, Ellen. "Political Communication and the Soviet Media Structure," in Joseph L. Nogee, ed., *Soviet Politics: Russia after Brezhnev.* New York: Praeger Press, 1984.

————. *Media and the Russian Republic.* New York: Praeger Press, 1981.

Middleton, Harry J. *The Compact History of the Korean War.* New York: Hawthorn Books, Inc., 1965.

Miers, Earl N. *The American Story.* New York: Channel Press, 1956.

Mikhailov, N. *Soviet Russia.* New York: Sheridan House, 1948.

Miller, David. *Modern Submarines.* New York: Arco Publishing, Inc., 1982.

Miller, D.M.O., et al. *The Balance of Military Power.* New York: Salamander Books, 1981.

Miller, Jay. *Convair 5-58.* Arlington, Tex.: Aerofax Inc., 1985.

Morison, Samuel Eliot. *The Oxford History of the American People*. New York: Oxford University Press, 1965.

Morris, Charles R. *Iron Destinies, Lost Opportunities*. New York: Harper & Row, 1988.

Mosyaikin, V.V. *The Dosaaf Orgnanization: Programme of Action*. Moscow: DOSAAF Publishers, 1978.

Mstislavskii, Sergei. *Five Days Which Transformed Russia*. London: The Second World, 1988.

Mueller, John. *Retreat from Doomsday*. New York: Basic Books, Inc., 1989.

Myagkov, A. *Inside the KGB*. New York: Ballantine Books, 1981.

Nash, Roderick. *From These Beginnings*. New York: Harper & Row, 1978.

Nemzer, L. *Basic Patterns of Political and Propaganda Operations in the Soviet Armed Forces*. Chevy Chase, Md.: Johns Hopkins University Press, 1953.

New Age Encyclopedia. Lexicon Press: Phillipines, 1979.

Newhouse, John. *Cold Dawn—The Story of SALT*. Washington: Pergamon-Brassey's, 1989.

————. *JFK and Vietnam*. New York: Warner Books, 1992.

Noonan, Peggy. *What I Saw at the Revolution*. New York: Random House, 1990.

Parmet, Herbert S. *Nixon and His America*. Boston: Little, Brown & Co., 1990.

Patterson, Bradley H., Jr. *The Ring of Power*. New York: Basic Books, Inc., 1988.

Payne, James L. *The American Threat: The Fear of War as an Instrument of Foreign Policy*. Chicago: Markham Publishing Co., 1970.

Penkovsky, Oleg. *The Penkovsky Papers*. Translated by Peter Deriabin. New York: Avon Books, 1965.

Polmar, Norman, and Timothy M. Laur. *Strategic Air Command*. Baltimore: The Nautical & Aviation Publishing Company of America, 1990.

Pipes, Richard. *U.S. – Soviet Relations in the Era of Détente*. Boulder, Colo.: Westview Press, 1981.

Polmar, Norman. *Atomic Submarines*. Princeton, N.J.: Van Nostrand, 1963.

————. *Death of the Thresher.* Philadelphia: Chilton Books, 1964.

————. *Rickover.* New York: Simon & Schuster, 1982.

Polyaakov, Y. *A History of Soviet Society.* Moscow: Progress Publishers, 1977.

Power, Gen Thomas S. *USAF: Design for Survival.* New York: Pocket Books, 1965.

Powers, Francis Gary, with Curt Gentry. *Operation Overflight.* New York: Holt, Rinehart & Winston, 1970.

Prados, John. *The Soviet Estimate.* New York: The Dial Press, 1982.

————. *Presidents' Secret Wars.* New York: William Morrow & Co., Inc., 1986.

Pringle, Peter, and William Arkin. *SIOP.* New York: W.W. Norton & Co., 1984.

Rhodes, Richard. *The Making of the Atomic Bomb.* New York: Simon & Schuster, 1986.

Rowan, Henry S., and Charles Wolf Jr. *The Impoverished Superpower: Perestrokia and the Soviet Military Burden.* San Francisco: ICS Press, 1989.

Rubinstein, Alvin Z. *Soviet Foreign Policy Since World War II, Imperial and Global.* Cambridge, Mass.: Winthrop Publishers, Inc., 1981.

Sagan, Scott. *The Limits of Safety.* Princeton, N. J.: Princeton University Press, 1993.

Schick, Jack. *The Berlin Crisis,1958–1962.* Philadelphia: University of Pennsylvania Press, 1971.

Schlesinger, Arthur M. *The Imperial Presidency.* Boston: Houghton Mifflin, 1973.

————. *The Cycles of American History.* Boston: Houghton Mifflin, 1986.

Schuman, Frederick L. *The Cold War Retrospect and Prospect.* Baton Rouge: Louisiana State University Press, 1962.

Scott, W. F., and H. F. Scott. *Armed Forces of the USSR.* New York: Westview, 1983.

Sevy, Grace. *The American Experience in Vietnam.* Norman, Okla.: University of Oklahoma Press, 1989.

Shipler, David K. *Russia: Broken Idols, Solemn Dreams.* New York: Penguin Books, 1989.

Shultz, Richard H., and Roy Godson, *Dezinformatsia–Active Measures in the Soviet Strategy.* Washington, D.C.: Pergamon-Brassey's, 1984.

Singer, J. David. *Deterrence, Arms Control, and Disarmament.* Columbus, Ohio: Ohio State University Press, 1962.

Skirdo, M. P. *The People, The Army, The Commander.* Moscow: Military Publishing House, 1970.

Skousen, W. Cleon. *The Naked Russian.* Salt Lake City, Utah: The Ensign Publishing Co., 1960.

Slessor, Sir John. *Strategy for the West.* New York: William Morrow & Co., 1954.

Smith, Bruce L. R. *The RAND Corporation.* Cambridge: Harvard University Press, 1966.

Smith, Hedrick. *The New Russians.* New York: Random House, 1990.

Smith, Joseph B. *Portrait of a Cold Warrior.* New York: Putnam's, 1976.

Smolen, Rick, and David Cohen (Project Directors). *A Day in the Life of the Soviet Union.* New York: Collins Publishers, Inc, 1987.

Smorigo, N. I. *Towards More Effective Propaganda and Agitation.* Moscow: Military Publishing House, 1979.

Snyder, Glenn H. *Deterrence and Defense: Toward a Theory of National Security.* Princeton, N. J.: Princeton University Press, 1961.

Snyder, William P., and James Brown. *Defense Policy in the Reagan Administration.* Washington, D.C.: National Defense University Report, 1988.

Sorenson, Theodore C. *Kennedy.* New York: Harper & Row Publishers, 1965.

Soviet Aerospace Handbook. Washington, D.C.: Translated by the US Air Force, 1978.

Spielman, Karl F. *Analyzing Soviet Strategic Arms Decisions.* Boulder, Colo.: Westview Press, 1978.

Steele, Jonathan. *Soviet Power: The Kremlin's Foreign Policy - Brezhnev to Chernenko.* New York: Simon & Schuster, Inc., 1984.

Stockman, David A. *The Triumph of Politics.* New York: Avon, 1987.

Sulzberger, C. L. *A Long Row of Candles.* Toronto: MacMillan Co., 1969.

Suvorov, Viktor. *Inside the Soviet Army.* New York: MacMillan Publishing Co., Inc., 1982.

———. *Spetsnaz.* New York: W.W. Norton & Co., 1987.

Tarasulo, Isaac J., *Perils of Perestroika.* Wilmington, Del.: S. R. Books, 1992.

Taylor, Gen Maxwell D. USA, Retired. *Responsibility and Response.* New York: Harper & Row, 1967.

———. *The Uncertain Trumpet.* New York: Harper & Brothers, 1959.

Taylor, William J., and Steven A. Taylor. *The Future of Conflict in the 1980s.* Lexington, Mass.: Lexington Books, 1982.

Tindall, George Brown. *America–A Narrative History.* New York: W. W. Norton, 1984.

Tobenkin, Elias. *Stalin's Ladder.* New York: Minton, Balch & Co., 1933.

Toffler, Alvin, and Heidi Toffler. *War and Anti-War.* New York: Little, Brown & Co., 1993.

Tocqueville, Alexis de. *Democracy in America.* Edited and abridged by Richard D. Heffner. New York: New American Library, 1956.

Tyler, Patrick. *Running Critical.* New York: Harper & Row Publishers, 1986.

Tyson, James L. *Target America: The Influence of Communist Propaganda on US Media.* Chicago: Regnery Gateway, 1981.

Vernadsky, George. *A History of Russia.* New Haven: Yale University Press, 1974.

Volkogonov, D.A. *Handbook for Progagandists and Agitators in the Army and the Fleet.* Moscow: Military Publishing House, 1978.

Voskresenskaya, L. A. *A Word About a Great Matter.* Moscow: Children's Press, 1981.

Watts, Robert B. *Dynamic Freedoms.* Washington, D. C.: The Supreme Council, Scottish Rite of Freemasonry, Undated.

Weisberger, Bernard A. *Cold War Cold Peace.* New York: Houghton Mifflin Co., 1985.

Wise, David, and Thomas B. Ross. *The U-2 Affair.* New York: Random House, 1962.

Williams, E. S. *The Soviet Military*. New York: St. Martin's Press, 1986.

Wells, H. G. *The Outline of History*. New York: Doubleday, 1949.

Wettig, Gerhard. *High Road, Low Road: Diplomacy & Public Action in Soviet Foreign Policy*. Washington, D.C.: Pergamon-Brassey's International Defense Publishers, 1989.

Wolfe, Alan. *The Rise and Fall of the Soviet Threat*. Washington, D.C.: Institute of Policy Studies, 1979.

Yenne, Bill. *SAC: A Primer of Modern Strategic Airpower*. Novato, Calif.: Presidio Press, 1985.

Yergin, Daniel. *Shattered Peace: The Origins of the Cold War and the National Security*. Boston: Houghton Mifflin, 1978.

York, Herbert F. *The Advisors: Oppenheimer, Teller and the Superbomb*. San Francisco: W. H. Freeman, 1976.

Published Reports

Alert Operations and the Straategic Air Command 1957–1991. Office of the Historian, Headquarters SAC. Offutt AFB, Nebraska, 7 December 1991.

Bohn, John T. *A Conversation with LeMay*. Office of the Historian, SAC, Offutt AFB, Nebraska, November 1972.

Conversino, Mark J., Maj. USAF. *Back to the Stone Age: The Attack on Curtis E. LeMay*. Paper presented at America's Shield Symposium, Offutt AFB, 15–17 May 1996.

Hopkins, Charles K. *Unclassified History of the Joint Strategic Target Planning Staff (JSTPS)*. Offutt AFB, Nebraska, 26 June 1990.

Peck, Earl G. *B-47 Stratojet, Aerospace Historian*, vol. 22, no. 2. Manhattan, Kans.: Department of History, Kansas State University, June 1975.

US Air Force Almanac Issue, 1997, 1978, 1981. Air Force Magazine. Washington, D.C.

Periodicals

Alexander, George. "Life With the Minuteman," *Newsweek*, 7 April 1969.

Alsop, Joseph. "The New Balance of Power," *Encounter Magazine,* vol. 10, no. 5, May 1958.

Alsop, Stewart. "How Can we Catch up?," *Saturday Evening Post,* vol. 230, no. 24, 14 December 1957.

Austin, Harold (Hal). "A Cold War Overflight of the USSR," *Daedalus Flyer,* Spring 1995.

Bialer, Seweryn. "Gorbachev's Move," *Foreign Policy,* no. 68, Fall 1987.

Bivens, Matt. "MM Report: Russian Roulette," *Modern Maturity,* vol., 37, no. 5, September–October 1994.

Bruz, V. "The Brainwashing of USAAF Crews," *Air Defence Herald.* Moscow: July 1981.

Chelminski, Rudolph. "Last Mystery of the CZAR," *Reader's Digest.* December 1995.

Duffy, Brian, and Edward T. Pound. "The Million Dollar Spy," *US News & World Report.* vol. 116, no. 9, 7 March 1994.

Edmundson, James V. Lt Gen, USAF, Retired. "Six Churning and Four Burning," three-part series. *Klaxon Magazine.* Omaha, Nebraska, vol. 3, Issues 3 and 4, vol. 4, Issue 1, 1995-1996.

Garthoff, Raymond. "Russia—Leading the World in ICBM and Satellite Development," *Missiles and Rockets,* vol. 2, no. 12, October 1957.

Gartner, Michael. "News Languishing Without Passion," *USA Today.* 8 October 1996.

Gray, Colin S. "Detente, Arms Control and Strategy: Perspectives on Salt," *American Political Science Review,* vol. 70, no. 4, December 1976.

Horne, Alistair. "The Worst Military Decisions of the Twentieth Century—Advance to the Yalu." FYI Supplement to *Forbes Magazine,* 1995.

Kaufman, Robert "Yogi," Vice Adm USN, Retired and Steve Kaufman. "The Silent Service," *The Retired Officer Magazine.* Washington, D.C., February 1995.

Murray, Stanley H. "Treasures of the CZARS," *The Retired Officer Magazine,* vol. L, no. 10, October 1994.

Parshall, Gerald. "Special Report: Shock Wave," *U.S. News & World Report,* vol. 119, no. 5, 31 July 1995.

Pratt, Colonel Henry J. "The Buck Stops Here," *The Retired Officer Magazine*, vol. LI, no. 4, April 1995.

Rhodes, Richard. "The General and World War III," *The New Yorker*. New York, 19 June 1995.

Roberts, Steven, et al. "Why There Are Still Spies," *U.S. News & World Report*, vol.116, no. 9, 7 March 1994.

Sagan, Scott. "Nuclear Alerts and Crisis Management," *International Security*, vol. 9.

"Soviet Pilot Says He Downed U-2 'Unarmed'," *Plane Talk*. Employee Publication of Lockheed Martin Tactical Aircraft Systems, vol. 4, no. 18, 22 October 1996.

Sowell, Thomas, "An Unnecessary War," *Forbes Magazine*, vol. 158, no. 10, August 1995.

Stanglin, Douglas, et al., "Special Report: The End of the Empire," *U.S. News & World Report*, vol. 111, no. 11, 9 September 1991.

Thoenes, Sander, and Alan Cooperman. "Yelstin's Eyes and Ears," *U.S. News & World Report*, vol. 119, no. 6, 7 August 1995.

Voskresenskaya, L. A. "What they teach Tommy," *Red Star*, 24 January 1977.

———. "Who Would like to Become an Officer?," *Red Star*, 19 January 1982.

Documentaries

Lashmar, Paul, executive producer. "Baiting the Bear," *Time Watch Series*, British Broadcasting Co., 1996.

Reports

Adams, Christopher S. Research Report, "Doing Business in the Newly Independent Nations," 15 September 1992.

Index

☆U.S. GOVERNMENT PRINTING OFFICE:1999-738-168/00088